United States Government Accountability Office

Report to the Caucus on International Narcotics Control, U.S. Senate

I0448669

September 2013

CENTRAL AMERICA

U.S. Agencies Considered Various Factors in Funding Security Activities, but Need to Assess Progress in Achieving Interagency Objectives

GAO Highlights

Highlights of GAO-13-771, a report to the Caucus on International Narcotics Control, U.S. Senate

CENTRAL AMERICA

U.S. Agencies Considered Various Factors in Funding Security Activities, but Need to Assess Progress in Achieving Interagency Objectives

Why GAO Did This Study

Drug trafficking organizations and gangs have expanded in Central America, threatening the security of these countries and the United States. Since 2008, the U.S. government has helped Central America and Mexico respond to these threats and in 2010 established CARSI solely to assist Central America. CARSI's goals are to create safe streets, disrupt criminals and contraband, support capable governments, and increase state presence and cooperation among CARSI partners. GAO reported on CARSI funding in January 2013 and was asked to further review CARSI and related activities in Central America.

This report (1) provides an updated assessment of U.S. agencies' funding and activities that support CARSI goals; (2) examines whether U.S. agencies took steps to consider partner country needs, absorptive capacities, and U.S. and non-U.S. investments when selecting CARSI activities; and (3) examines information on the extent to which U.S. agencies reported CARSI results and evaluated CARSI activities. GAO analyzed CARSI and complementary non-CARSI funding; reviewed documents on CARSI activities, partner country needs, and CARSI results; interviewed U.S. agency officials about CARSI and related activities; and observed CARSI activities in three countries.

What GAO Recommends

GAO recommends that State and USAID work with other agencies to assess progress in achieving the objectives of the interagency strategy for Central America. State and USAID concurred with the recommendation.

View GAO-13-771. For more information, contact Charles Michael Johnson, Jr., at (202) 512-7331 or JohnsonCM@gao.gov.

What GAO Found

Since fiscal year 2008, U.S. agencies allocated over $1.2 billion in funding for Central America Regional Security Initiative (CARSI) activities and non-CARSI funding that supports CARSI goals. As of June 1, 2013, the Department of State (State) and the United States Agency for International Development (USAID) obligated at least $463 million of the close to $495 million in allocated funding for CARSI activities, and disbursed at least $189 million to provide partner countries with equipment, technical assistance, and training to improve interdiction and disrupt criminal networks. Moreover, as of March 31, 2013, U.S. agencies estimated that they had allocated approximately $708 million in non-CARSI funding that supports CARSI goals, but data on disbursements were not readily available. U.S. agencies, including State, the Department of Defense (DOD), and the Department of Justice, use this funding to provide equipment, technical assistance, and training, as well as infrastructure and investigation assistance to partner countries. For example, DOD allocated $25 million in funding to help Guatemala establish an interagency border unit to combat drug trafficking.

State and USAID took a variety of steps—using assessment reports, outreach meetings with host governments and other donors, and interagency meetings—to help identify and consider partner countries' needs, absorptive capacities, and related U.S. and non-U.S. investments when selecting CARSI activities. For example, State used an assessment report on crime scene investigation and forensic programs and capacities of six partner countries to inform decisions on selecting CARSI activities. In addition, USAID officials used assessment reports to help identify and consider partner country juvenile justice and community policing needs and absorptive capacities; these assessment reports included specific recommendations for designing and selecting juvenile justice and community policing projects in partner countries. Also, in one partner country, embassy officials used donor outreach meetings to identify another donor's significant investment in police intelligence in the partner country; the embassy consequently reduced funding for CARSI activities in that area.

While U.S. agencies have reported on some CARSI results, they have not assessed progress in meeting interagency objectives for Central America. State and USAID have reported some CARSI results through various mechanisms at the initiative, country, and project levels. For example, one embassy reported that its CARSI-supported anti-gang education project had expanded nationwide and taught over 3,000 children over 3 years of the program. However, U.S. agencies have not assessed their performance using the metrics outlined in a 2012 interagency strategy for Central America that were designed to measure the results of CARSI and related non-CARSI activities. GAO recognizes that collecting performance data may be challenging and that the metrics could require some adjustments. Nevertheless, assessing progress toward achieving the strategy's objectives could help guide U.S. agencies' decisions about their activities and identify areas for improvement. In addition to ongoing assessments of progress, GAO has concluded in prior work that evaluations are important to obtain more in-depth information on programs' performance and context. USAID is conducting an evaluation of its CARSI crime prevention programming to be completed in 2014. State officials said that they are planning to conduct an evaluation of some of their CARSI activities beginning in fiscal year 2014.

_____ United States Government Accountability Office

Contents

Tables

Figures

Abbreviations

CARSI	Central America Regional Security Initiative
CBP	Customs and Border Protection
CT	Counterterrorism
DEA	Drug Enforcement Administration
DHS	Department of Homeland Security
DOD	Department of Defense
DOJ	Department of Justice
DSCA	Defense Security Cooperation Agency
DFAS	Defense Financing and Accounting Service
ESF	Economic Support Fund
EXBS	Export Control and Related Border Security
FMF	Foreign Military Financing
IAWG	Central America Interagency Working Group
IDB	Inter-American Development Bank
INCLE	International Narcotics Control and Law Enforcement
INL	Bureau of International Narcotics and Law Enforcement Affairs
NADR	Nonproliferation, Anti-terrorism, Demining, and Related Programs
State	Department of State
Treasury	Department of the Treasury
USAID	United States Agency for International Development
WHA	Bureau of Western Hemisphere Affairs

GAO U.S. GOVERNMENT ACCOUNTABILITY OFFICE

441 G St. N.W.
Washington, DC 20548

September 25, 2013

The Honorable Dianne Feinstein
Chairman
The Honorable Charles Grassley
Co-Chairman
Caucus on International Narcotics Control
United States Senate

In recent years, the security situation in Central America has deteriorated as drug trafficking organizations, gangs, and other criminal groups have expanded their activities, taking advantage of weak government institutions and poor social conditions. These groups have reportedly been able to operate with virtual impunity and the situation threatens both the stability and security of Central American countries, as well as the national security of the United States, as drugs, violence, and crime spread across borders. The U.S. government established the Mérida Initiative in 2008 to help Mexico and Central American countries respond to these threats. In 2010, the U.S. government established a new initiative, solely for Central American countries, called the Central America Regional Security Initiative (CARSI).[1] CARSI funds U.S. assistance activities in Belize, Costa Rica, El Salvador, Guatemala, Honduras, Nicaragua, and Panama (hereafter referred to as "partner countries").

The Department of State (State) and the United States Agency for International Development (USAID) both implement CARSI activities using an integrated approach to support judicial reform, community policing, and corrections efforts, as well as crime prevention, law enforcement, and counternarcotics programs. Given the range of challenges facing partner countries and limited U.S. resources, State and USAID pursue a mix of activities in an effort to maximize results and best achieve CARSI goals. U.S. agencies such as the Departments of Defense (DOD), Homeland Security (DHS), Justice (DOJ), and the Treasury (Treasury)—along with State and USAID—have also used non-CARSI funding to support complementary activities and programs in

---

[1]For the purposes of this review, the term CARSI will be used to refer to activities in Central America under the earlier Mérida Initiative, as well as under the more recent CARSI.

GAO-13-771 Central America

Central America. In 2012, the National Security Staff approved an interagency citizen security strategy for Central America designed to help coordinate and focus the U.S. government's CARSI and complementary non-CARSI activities in the region.

You asked us to review several issues related to CARSI. In January 2013, we issued a report with information on the status of funding for CARSI activities, including the amount that was disbursed to support partner countries during fiscal years 2008 through 2011, and information on amounts allocated, obligated, and disbursed by year of appropriation.[2] This report (1) provides an updated assessment of U.S. agencies' funding and activities that support CARSI goals; (2) examines whether U.S. agencies took steps to consider partner country needs, absorptive capacities, and related U.S. and non-U.S. investments when selecting activities to fund under CARSI; and (3) examines information on the extent to which U.S. agencies reported CARSI results and evaluated CARSI activities.[3]

To examine CARSI funding and activities, we collected data from State and USAID on funds allocated, obligated, and disbursed for CARSI activities from fiscal year 2008 through June 1, 2013, and reviewed documentation on CARSI-funded activities. As agencies may use slightly different funding terms, we provided them with definitions from GAO's *A Glossary of Terms Used in the Federal Budget Process* and worked with agencies to obtain data that met these definitions, to the extent possible.[4] In providing technical comments on a draft of this report, State officials reported an amount of almost $10.6 million in additional International

---

[2]GAO, *Status of Funding for the Central America Regional Security Initiative,* GAO-13-295R (Washington, D.C.: Jan. 30, 2013). While reviewing a draft of this report, State identified additional funds that it had allocated to CARSI in fiscal year 2010. We have incorporated these new data in this report; therefore, the CARSI funding information in our January 2013 report is superseded by the information in this report.

[3]For the purposes of this report, we define partner country needs as gaps in a partner country's citizen security that could be addressed with the help of U.S. assistance. Absorptive capacity is the ability of the partner country to receive and effectively utilize U.S. assistance. Related U.S. investments are non-CARSI investments that promote citizen security from any U.S. agency. Related non-U.S. investments are investments that promote citizen security from other donor governments, international organizations, and from the partner country itself.

[4]GAO, *A Glossary of Terms Used in the Federal Budget Process,* GAO-05-734SP (Washington, D.C.: Sept. 2005).

Narcotics Control and Law Enforcement (INCLE) funding that was allocated for CARSI activities in fiscal year 2010 that had not been previously reported to GAO. State officials also said that they could not provide obligation or disbursement information related to this amount because these INCLE funds are centrally managed and State's financial systems do not allow them to track such funds by region or country. According to State officials, that is why these funds were not previously reported to GAO. We confirmed with State officials that the funds had been applied to CARSI activities and documented the programs toward which the funds had been applied. Although State officials were not able to track the obligation or disbursement of these funds, we have included this amount in the total allocated for CARSI activities. We made note of this discrepancy in presenting these data in the report. To examine non-CARSI funding and activities that support CARSI goals, we collected data and reviewed documentation on non-CARSI activities from State and USAID, as well as DOD, DOJ, DHS, and Treasury, for fiscal year 2008 through the first half of fiscal year 2013. To assess the reliability of the CARSI and non-CARSI data provided, we requested and reviewed information from agency officials regarding the underlying financial data systems and the checks, controls, and reviews used to generate the data and ensure their accuracy and reliability. We found the data sufficiently reliable for our purposes. At the time of reporting, the most recent data available on funding for CARSI were as of June 1, 2013, and the most recent non-CARSI funding data available were as of March 31, 2013. However, we found no change in the total CARSI allocations between March 31, 2013, and June 1, 2013. Thus, it is possible to compare CARSI and non-CARSI funding allocations.

To examine steps U.S. agencies used to help identify and consider key factors when selecting activities to fund under CARSI, we reviewed documentation from State and USAID, including U.S. agency assessments of partner countries, as well as written statements provided to us from embassies in partner countries and from State and USAID on the steps they utilized. To examine the extent to which U.S. agencies reported CARSI results and evaluated CARSI activities, we reviewed State, USAID, and other agencies' documentation on CARSI activities and the results of these activities. We also compared U.S. agencies' actions to assess and report their progress toward achieving the objectives in the interagency strategy for Central America against key considerations that we identified in 2012 for implementing interagency collaboration mechanisms.[5] In our previous work, we found that one key feature in the successful implementation of such mechanisms is the development of a system for monitoring and reporting on results. In addition, we compared agencies' activities against leading practices GAO identified in 1996 for performance management of federal programs.[6]

To support work on all three objectives, we conducted interviews with State, USAID, DOD, DOJ (and its components), DHS (and its components), and Treasury officials in Washington, D.C. In addition, we visited three partner countries—Belize, Guatemala, and Panama. We selected these three countries as a sample considering the following elements—the scope of the citizen security problem; the amount of funding for CARSI activities received from fiscal year 2008 to 2012; the range of CARSI activities undertaken; the extent of non-CARSI U.S. government activities that support CARSI objectives; and the extent of host government or other donor citizen security efforts in these countries. In these three countries, we met with U.S. agency officials as well as host government, international organization, and other donor government officials. We also visited CARSI and non-CARSI activity locations during these visits. For additional details about our scope and methodology, see appendix I.

We conducted this performance audit from August 2012 to September 2013 in accordance with generally accepted government auditing standards. Those standards require that we plan and perform the audit to obtain sufficient, appropriate evidence to provide a reasonable basis for our findings and conclusions based on our audit objectives. We believe that the evidence obtained provides a reasonable basis for our findings and conclusions based on our audit objectives.

---

[5]We developed this list of considerations through a review of relevant literature on collaboration mechanisms, interviews with experts on collaboration, and a review of findings from a number of our previous reports on collaboration in the federal government. See GAO, *Managing for Results: Key Considerations for Implementing Interagency Collaborative Mechanisms*, GAO-12-1022 (Washington, D.C.: Sept. 27, 2012).

[6]We developed this list of practices through the study of the experiences of leading public sector organizations, a review of management studies of federal agencies, and interviews with federal executives and other experts on performance management. See GAO, *Executive Guide: Effectively Implementing the Government Performance and Results Act*, GAO/GGD-96-118 (Washington, D.C.: June 1996).

Background

The security situation in Central America has continued to deteriorate in recent years as Mexican drug trafficking organizations, transnational gangs, and other criminal groups have expanded their activities, contributing to escalating levels of crime and violence. Violence is particularly high in the "northern triangle" countries of El Salvador, Guatemala, and Honduras, with homicide rates among the highest in the world. Efforts to counter illicit trafficking in Colombia and Mexico created an environment that became increasingly inhospitable to drug trafficking organizations, forcing criminal groups to displace operations into Central America where they could exploit institutional weaknesses. Recognizing this situation, the United States has sought to develop collaborative security partnerships with Central American countries. As part of this effort, in 2010 the United States split off the Central America portion of the Mérida Initiative and established a new initiative named CARSI.[7] According to State, CARSI is designed as a collaborative partnership between the United States and Central American partner countries. Its focus is on improving citizen security within the region, taking a broad approach to the issues of security beyond traditional counternarcotics activities. Figure 1 shows the CARSI partner countries in Central America.

---

[7]In 2008, the United States established the Mérida Initiative, a multiyear assistance package to Mexico and Central America, to help address increasing violence and criminal activity, especially from drug-trafficking and other criminal organizations.

Figure 1: Map of Central America Regional Security Initiative Partner Countries and Neighboring Countries

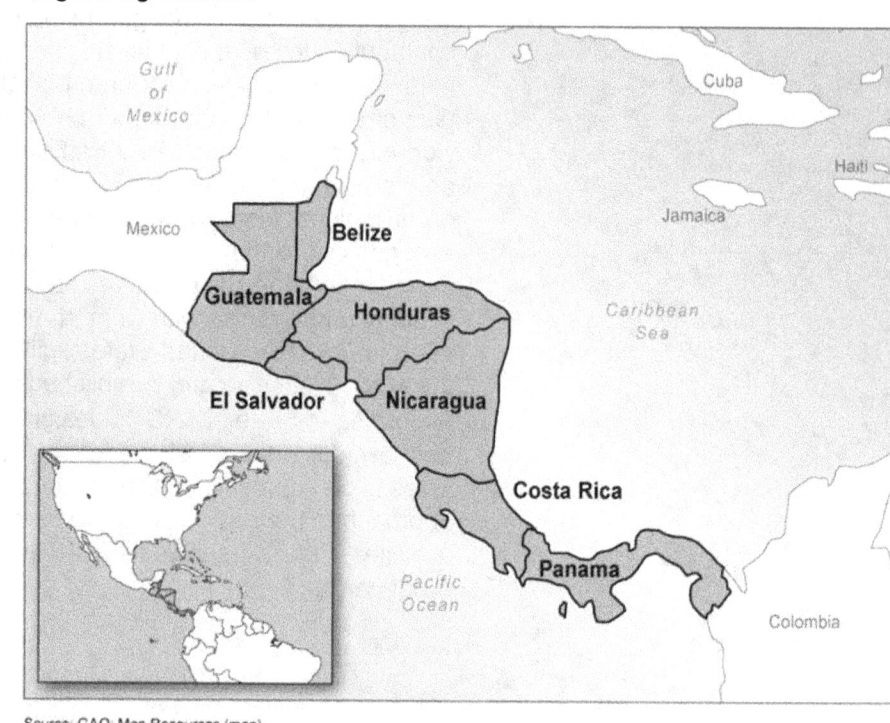

Source: GAO; Map Resources (map).

According to State, CARSI's five primary goals are to

- create safe streets for citizens in the region;
- disrupt the movement of criminals and contraband to, within, and between the nations of Central America;
- support the development of strong, capable, and accountable Central American governments;
- re-establish effective state presence and security in communities at risk; and
- foster enhanced levels of security coordination and cooperation among nations in the region.

Funding for CARSI activities has come from a combination of four U.S. foreign assistance accounts—the INCLE account; the Economic Support Fund (ESF) account; the Nonproliferation, Anti-Terrorism, Demining, and Related Programs (NADR) account; and the Foreign Military Financing (FMF) account. General descriptions of how these accounts are used globally are provided below.

Generally,

- the INCLE account is used to provide assistance to foreign countries and international organizations to assist them in developing and implementing policies and programs that maintain the rule of law and strengthen institutional law enforcement and judicial capabilities, including countering drug flows and combating transnational crime;
- the ESF account is used to assist foreign countries in meeting their political, economic, and security needs by funding a range of activities, including those designed to counter terrorism and extremist ideology, increase the role of the private sector in the economy, develop effective legal systems, build transparent and accountable governance, and empower citizens;
- the NADR account is used to fund contributions to certain organizations supporting nonproliferation, and provides assistance to foreign countries for nonproliferation, demining, antiterrorism, export control assistance, and other related activities; and
- the FMF account is used to provide grants to foreign governments and international organizations for the acquisition of U.S. defense equipment, services, and training to enhance the capacity of foreign security forces.[8]

State manages the INCLE, NADR, and FMF accounts, and shares responsibility with USAID to manage and administer the ESF account. Within State, the Bureau for International Narcotics and Law Enforcement Affairs (INL) administers the INCLE account. The Bureau of Political-Military Affairs administers the FMF account, while DOD oversees the actual procurement and transfer of goods and services purchased with these funds. State's Bureau of International Security and Nonproliferation and its Bureau of Counterterrorism administer their NADR subaccounts. State's Bureau of Western Hemisphere Affairs administers a portion of ESF. However, USAID oversees the implementation of most CARSI programs funded from ESF. State's Bureau of Educational and Cultural Affairs also previously administered a onetime use of ESF funds for CARSI activities.

---

[8]Pursuant to appropriations for FMF, funding for FMF grants is obligated upon apportionment. According to State officials, though FMF may be used to provide loans as well as grants, it is rarely used in this manner.

State's Bureau of Western Hemisphere Affairs (WHA) has the lead within State for integrating CARSI activities with State's broader policy of promoting citizen security in Central America. State's primary funding source for CARSI activities is the INCLE account and the ESF account is USAID's primary funding source for CARSI activities. In addition to State and USAID, a number of other U.S. agencies use non-CARSI funding to implement activities in Central America that address various aspects of promoting citizen security that complement CARSI activities—including improving law enforcement and the criminal justice system, promoting rule of law and human rights, enhancing customs and border control, and encouraging economic and social development. DOD, DOJ, DHS, and Treasury are the key agencies involved in these non-CARSI funded activities.

U.S. Agencies Have Allocated Over $1.2 Billion in CARSI and Non-CARSI Funds to Support Various Security Activities in Central America

Since fiscal year 2008, U.S. agencies have allocated more than $1.2 billion in funding for CARSI activities and non-CARSI funding that supports CARSI goals.[9] As of June 1, 2013, State and USAID had allocated close to $495 million[10] and disbursed at least $189 million in funding for CARSI activities to provide partner countries with equipment, technical assistance, and training to improve interdiction and disrupt criminal networks.[11] As of March 31, 2013, U.S. agencies (State, USAID, DOD, DOJ, and DHS) estimated that they had also allocated approximately $708 million in non-CARSI funding that supports CARSI goals. U.S. agencies, including State, DOD, and DOJ, have used non-CARSI funding to provide additional security-related equipment, technical assistance, and training, as well as infrastructure and investigation assistance to the region. Data on disbursements of non-CARSI funding were not readily available for some agencies because of the complexity and challenges associated with how these agencies track their disbursement data. At the time of reporting, the most recent data available on funding for CARSI were as of June 1, 2013 and the most recent non-CARSI funding data available were as of March 31, 2013. However, we found no change in the total CARSI allocations between March 31, 2013 and June 1, 2013. Thus, it is possible to compare CARSI and non-CARSI funding allocations.

---

[9]For the purposes of this report, an allocation is a further subdivision by an agency of an apportionment, which is the method by which the Office of Management and Budget distributes amounts available for obligation. See GAO-05-734SP.

[10]State and USAID allocated close to $495 million for CARSI activities from the $496.5 million in appropriated funds designated for Central America from fiscal year 2008 to fiscal year 2012. According to State officials, in fiscal year 2009, $17 million in appropriated FMF funds was allocated for Central America, but State reprogrammed approximately $2 million due to policy restrictions related to a coup in Honduras and withheld funds from Nicaragua because certain reporting requirements were not met. State officials note that the approximately $2 million in reprogrammed funds account for the difference between the amount of appropriated funds that State reports to Congress as being designated for Central America and the total amount identified as allocated for CARSI activities.

[11]After reviewing a draft of this report, State officials reported an amount of almost $10.6 million in INCLE funding that was allocated for CARSI activities in fiscal year 2010 that had not been previously reported to GAO. State officials also said that they could not provide obligation or disbursement information related to this amount because these INCLE funds are centrally managed and State's financial systems do not allow them to track such funds by region or country. According to State officials, that is why these funds were not previously reported to GAO. Although State officials were not able to account for the obligation or disbursement of these funds, we have included this amount in the total of the close to $495 million allocated for CARSI activities.

State and USAID Have Obligated the Majority of the Close to $495 Million Allocated for CARSI since Fiscal Year 2008

As of June 1, 2013, State and USAID had allocated close to $495 million in funding for CARSI activities; the same amount had been allocated as of March 31, 2013, the time frame we use later to report on non-CARSI funding allocations. State and USAID have obligated at least $463 million of the close to $495 million allocated, and have disbursed at least $189 million of the allocated CARSI funds from the INCLE, ESF, and NADR accounts for activities in partner countries.[12] State and USAID disbursed funds to support activities in partner countries that improve law enforcement and maritime interdiction capabilities, support capacity building and training activities, prevent crime and violence, and deter and detect border criminal activity. After reviewing a draft of this report, State officials reported an amount of almost $10.6 million in INCLE funding that was allocated for CARSI activities in fiscal year 2010 that had not been previously reported to GAO. State officials also said that they could not provide obligation or disbursement information related to this amount because these INCLE funds are centrally managed and State's financial systems do not allow them to track such funds by region or country. According to State officials, this is why these funds were not previously reported to GAO. Although State officials were not able to track the obligation or disbursement of these funds, we have included this amount in the total of the close to $495 million allocated for CARSI activities.

Of the seven partner countries, the largest amounts of CARSI funds were allocated to Guatemala, Honduras, and El Salvador. In addition, 17 percent of the total allocations was for regional activities; that is, region-wide activities in Central America that are not tied to an activity in a specific country. Table 1 provides a breakdown of allocated, obligated, and disbursed funds for CARSI activities by country. To demonstrate how funding for CARSI activities has been allocated, obligated, and disbursed by year of appropriation, we are providing this information by account and by country in appendix II. In addition, we present data on how funding for CARSI activities under FMF have been allocated and committed by year of appropriation in appendix III.

---

[12]Because State was unable to provide a breakout of almost $10.6 million in INCLE funds, total allocations of $484 million, which excludes this amount, were used to make comparisons against obligations and disbursements.

Table 1: Total U.S. Funds Allocated, Obligated, and Disbursed to Support Central America Regional Security Initiative (CARSI) Activities, by Country, as of June 1, 2013

Dollars in thousands

Country	Allocated	Unobligated balance	Unliquidated obligations	Disbursed
Guatemala	111,190	1,005	65,142	43,669
Regional[a]	86,484	16,264	29,431	40,789
Honduras	85,531	150	58,589	25,276
El Salvador	80,846	2	40,941	31,029
Panama	51,601	949	20,517	25,565
Costa Rica	34,110	1,004	16,730	11,487
Belize	19,397	530	9,736	5,954
Nicaragua	14,817	1,367	6,287	5,629
INCLE Centrally Managed Account[b]	10,588	N/A	N/A	N/A
CARSI total[c]	**494,564**	**21,271**	**247,373**	**189,398**

Source: GAO analysis of State and USAID data.

Notes: Data are for fiscal year 2008 to June 1, 2013. Amounts have been rounded to the nearest thousand and therefore may not sum to totals. The allocation amounts did not change from March 31, 2013, to June 1, 2013. According to State and USAID officials, some of the unobligated balances from earlier fiscal years are no longer available for obligation. For the Foreign Military Financing (FMF) account, only allocations and unobligated balances are included; FMF unliquidated obligations and disbursements are not included because FMF funds are budgeted and tracked differently than funds from the other CARSI accounts and are not tracked consistent with our presentation of financial data.

[a]Regional amounts include funds from the International Narcotics Control and Law Enforcement; Economic Support Fund (State and USAID); and Nonproliferation, Anti-terrorism, Demining, and Related Programs accounts for "regional activities."

[b]State provided allocated amounts for CARSI activities from this account but was unable to provide information on the obligation or disbursement of these funds. According to State officials, these INCLE funds are centrally managed and are not tracked by region or country. Given that State was unable to provide a breakout of this almost $10.6 million in funds, total allocations of $484 million, which excludes this amount, were used to make comparisons against obligations and disbursements. N/A indicates that these data are not available.

[c]The total allocated amount does not equal the total combined sum of unobligated balances, unliquidated obligations, and disbursed because FMF funding is not included in unliquidated obligations and disbursements, and INCLE Centrally Management Account funding is not included in unobligated balance, unliquidated obligations, and disbursements.

Since we initially reported on CARSI in January 2013, the amount of funding for CARSI activities disbursed has increased from at least $75 million as of September 30, 2011, to at least $189 million as of June 1,

2013 from the INCLE, ESF, and NADR accounts.[13] According to State officials, disbursements increased because State took steps to alleviate delays associated with program administration in the implementation of CARSI (particularly in the early years), including an insufficient number of staff at embassies in partner countries to manage CARSI activities.[14] For example, in June 2013, the Assistant Secretary of State for INL reported in a congressional hearing that INL had increased staff positions in embassies in CARSI partner countries as INCLE funding represented about 64 percent of total CARSI allocations in these countries.[15] Currently, El Salvador, Guatemala, Honduras, and Panama have INL Sections (formerly known as Narcotics Affairs Sections); and Belize, Costa Rica, and Nicaragua have Narcotics Affairs Offices, according to State officials.[16] State and USAID have 5 years from the time the period of availability for obligation has expired to disburse funds.

State and USAID Fund Law Enforcement and Crime Prevention Activities in Partner Countries

State and USAID disbursed funds to support various activities in partner countries that improve law enforcement and maritime interdiction capabilities, support capacity building and training activities, prevent crime and violence, and deter and detect border criminal activity. However, there is a slight difference in emphasis between State and USAID in their CARSI-funded activities. State's efforts focus on capacity building of partner countries, while USAID's efforts focus on establishing prevention programs for at-risk youth in partner countries.

---

[13]GAO, *International Affairs: Status of Funding for the Central America Regional Security Initiative*, GAO-13-295R (Washington, D.C.: Jan. 30, 2013).

[14]GAO, *Mérida Initiative: The United States Has Provided Counternarcotics and Anticrime Support but Needs Better Performance Measures*, GAO-10-837 (Washington, D.C.: July 21, 2010). We previously found that U.S. agencies were working on various implementation challenges that contributed to implementation delays of Mérida-Central America. The cited delays included insufficient staff to administer programs, negotiations on interagency and bilateral agreements, procurement processes, changes in government, and funding availability.

[15]U.S. Congress, House Foreign Affairs Committee, Subcommittee on the Western Hemisphere, Regional Security Cooperation: Ambassador William R. Brownfield, Assistant Secretary of State for INL, *An Examination of the Central America Regional Security Initiative and the Caribbean Basin Security Initiative* (Washington, D.C.: June 19, 2013).

[16]Sections are fully funded with INL funds; Narcotics Affairs Offices, which are part of an embassy's Political Section, are partially funded with INL funds.

In general, State uses INCLE, ESF, FMF, and NADR funds to support activities such as

- strengthening the abilities of Central American law enforcement institutions to fight crime, violence, and trafficking in drugs and firearms;
- implementing high-impact, sustainable activities that focus on at-risk youth (such as job training and after school activities) and communities that are experiencing high levels of crime and violence;
- preventing the proliferation of advanced conventional weapons by helping to build effective national export control systems in countries that process, produce, or supply strategic items, as well as in countries through which such items are most likely to transit; and
- building and improving partner nation security force capacity to protect maritime borders and land territory against transnational threats such as illicit narcotics trafficking.

USAID uses ESF funds for CARSI activities in the following areas:

- services for at-risk youth, focusing on vocational training, job placement, after-school activities, community centers, and leadership development;
- municipal crime prevention activities, including community outreach for local police and support for crime observatories that coordinate data sharing to track crime statistics; and
- national and regional political reform activities to strengthen rule of law institutions and that reflect partner countries' commitments to reduce violence while creating the environment needed to institutionalize and sustain USAID efforts under CARSI.

Across the region, State and USAID use various CARSI-funded activities to carry out CARSI goals in each of the seven partner countries. Funding for CARSI activities provides partner countries with communication, border inspection, and security force equipment such as radios, computers, X-ray cargo scanners, narcotics identification kits, ballistic vests, and night-vision goggles. Funding for CARSI activities also provides related maintenance for this equipment. Figure 2 below shows examples of crime investigation forensic equipment and vehicles provided with funding for CARSI activities to the Belize Police Department.

Figure 2: Examples of Central America Regional Security Initiative (CARSI) Funded Equipment Provided to the Belize Police Department

 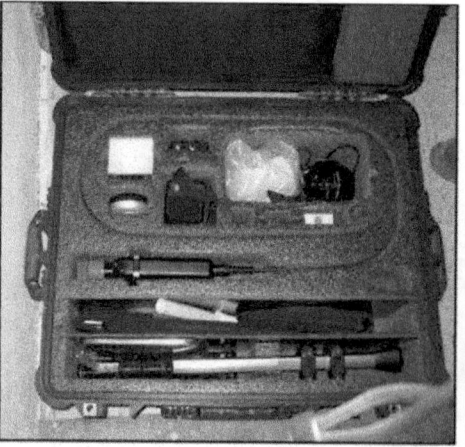 

Source: GAO.

In addition, funding for CARSI activities provides technical support and training to enhance partner countries' prosecutorial capabilities; management of courts, police academies, and prisons; and to support law enforcement operations (e.g., training to support narcotics interdiction). Funding for CARSI activities also provides support to partner countries to form specialized law enforcement units (also known as vetted units)[17] that are vetted by, and work with, U.S. personnel to investigate and disrupt the operations of transnational gangs and trafficking networks. Moreover, CARSI provides funding for partner countries to establish prevention activities designed to address underlying conditions (such as insufficient access to educational or economic opportunities and the prevalence of gangs) that leave communities vulnerable to crime and violence. Table 2 provides examples of CARSI activities in the seven partner countries.

---

[17]Vetted units are groups of partner country law enforcement officials who undergo background checks, including polygraph examinations. These vetted units conduct complex investigations in areas such as firearms and narcotics trafficking, gangs, bu k cash smuggling, and money laundering.

Table 2: Examples of Central America Regional Security Initiative (CARSI) Funded Activities in the Seven Partner Countries

CARSI partner country	CARSI funding account	CARSI-funded activities
Belize	State-INCLE	The Improved Borders activity provides targeted border security training, equipment, and technical assistance to Belize. It includes training on hidden compartments, fraudulent documents, and non-intrusive inspection equipment at border checkpoints and ports, and a newly established Mobile Interdiction Unit comprised of Belizean police, customs, and immigration officers.
Costa Rica	State-FMF	The Coast Guard Maritime Support activity focuses on enhancing the Costa Rican Coast Guard's maritime interdiction capabilities. This activity has provided two interdiction boats, associated equipment, operator training, and communication equipment to the Costa Rican Coast Guard.
El Salvador	State-INCLE	U.S. law enforcement mentors from the Drug Enforcement Administration, the Federal Bureau of Investigation, and Immigration and Customs Enforcement manage vetted units of El Salvador police and prosecutors to build these units' capacity to pursue complex investigations. For example, one vetted unit works with local El Salvadoran law enforcement personnel to identify gang structures, leadership, and infrastructure, and uses laws and investigative skills to disrupt gang operations. In the last quarter of 2012, this unit initiated a wiretap investigation that identified 30 members of a transnational extortion ring. In addition, according to U.S. law enforcement officials, this vetted unit has collected intelligence that has been used to convict criminals.
Guatemala	USAID-ESF	The Violence Prevention activity focuses on reducing the vulnerability of at-risk youth to gangs and criminal organizations, improving trust between police and community in target areas, and institutionalizing crime prevention policies at the national level. The activity has focused on the creation of Violence Prevention Commissions created by a joint task team of Guatemalan government officials and community leaders, and the development of Violence Prevention Plans by these commissions. These plans focus on gender issues and respond to community needs, such as education, work training, and increasing employment opportunities for young at-risk men and women.
Honduras	USAID-ESF	The Improving Education to Work, Learn, and Overcome activity provides at-risk youth living in areas vulnerable to drug trafficking and gangs with skills training. The activity creates alliances between Honduran organizations and the private sector to provide basic education and career readiness training to improve the preparation, competitiveness, and employability of at-risk youth.
Nicaragua	State-ESF	The Anti-Corruption activity aims to promote ethical behavior in the public and private sectors of society through education and awareness of corruption in its various forms throughout Nicaragua.
Panama	State-INCLE	The Police Reform activity works to build the capacity of Panamanian police units through training, mentoring, and the provision of equipment. The goal is for the Panamanian police to become a more modern, community-based police service that works within communities to effectively police and lower crime, while combating serious crimes such as drug trafficking, gangs, and money laundering. Police personnel receive training on police curriculum and criminal investigations, as well as on the Comparative Statistics (CompStat) activity designed to improve intelligence-led policing.[a]

Source: State and USA D.

Notes: INCLE is the International Narcotics Control and Law Enforcement account; FMF is the Foreign Military Financing account; ESF is the Economic Support Fund account; and USAID is the United States Agency for International Development.

[a]According to Embassy Panama officials, CompStat is being incorporated into the Panamanian National Police precincts and all police personnel were to be using the system as of July 1, 2013.

U.S. Agencies Have Allocated an Estimated $708 Million in Non-CARSI Funding since Fiscal Year 2008 for Various Activities That Supported CARSI Goals

As of March 31, 2013, U.S. agencies estimated that they had allocated approximately $708 million in non-CARSI funding that supported CARSI goals from fiscal year 2008 through the first half of fiscal year 2013, with State, USAID, and DOD allocating the largest amount of non-CARSI funds to support CARSI goals.[18] U.S. agencies (State, USAID, DOD, DOJ, and DHS) reported using their non-CARSI funding to implement a range of activities that supported CARSI goals, including providing training, technical assistance, equipment, infrastructure, and investigation and operational support to partner countries. To estimate the amount of non-CARSI assistance that has been allocated for partner countries that supported CARSI goals, we collected data from State and USAID as well as DOD, DOJ, DHS, and Treasury for fiscal year 2008 through the second quarter of fiscal year 2013. We did not report data on disbursements of non-CARSI funding because these data were not readily available for some agencies owing to the complexity and challenges associated with how these agencies track their disbursement data.

The allocated amount of non-CARSI funding supporting CARSI goals was 43 percent greater than the allocated amount of funds for CARSI activities, as of March 31, 2013. The largest share of non-CARSI funding was allocated to Honduras, Guatemala, and El Salvador, as shown in table 3.

---

[18]In collecting these data, we asked agencies to provide funding data for activities that they determined supported one or more of CARSI's five pillars. In addition, we asked agencies to provide only data on non-CARSI funding that directly assisted partner countries such as funding for training, equipment, infrastructure, and operational or investigative support. To avoid double-counting across agencies, we asked them to provide data on activities funded through their own appropriations. To the extent possible, we worked with the agencies to obtain uniform information and to minimize the risks of underestimating or overestimating the reported allocation amounts. In doing so, we worked with the agencies to make adjustments to the data they provided, as appropriate.

Table 3: Estimated U.S. Non-Central America Regional Security Initiative (CARSI) Funds Allocated That Support CARSI Goals, by Country, as of March 31, 2013

Dollars in thousands

Country	FY 2008	FY 2009	FY 2010	FY 2011	FY 2012	FY 2013 (first two quarters)	Total
Honduras	16,896	2,791	38,654	30,635	57,748	11,646	158,369
Guatemala	21,518	25,759	36,494	29,727	39,350	7,390	160,238
El Salvador	20,786	18,305	16,835	19,124	18,352	5,207	98,608
Panama	5,750	11,265	18,019	25,053	21,078	4,297	85,462
Regional[a]	14,292	12,110	7,541	15,117	11,490	0[b]	60,499
Nicaragua	12,946	9,400	18,783	18,643	9,289	8,960	78,022
Belize	2,670	1,325	11,554	8,007	8,470	2,111	34,136
Costa Rica	2,193	3,707	13,080	6,404	6,051	1,687	33,123
Non-CARSI total	**97,050**	**84,660**	**160,961**	**152,710**	**171,829**	**41,247**	**708,457**

Source: GAO analysis of DHS, DOJ, DOD, State, and USA D data.

Notes: Data are from fiscal year 2008 to the second quarter of fiscal year 2013. Non-CARSI reported amounts are from the Department of Homeland Security, Department of Justice, Department of Defense, Department of State, and United States Agency for International Development. Drug Enforcement Administration (DEA) data are not included in the Department of Justice data for fiscal years 2008 and 2009 because DEA transitioned to a new financial system during fiscal year 2009 and data for these years were not readily available, according to DEA officials. Amounts have been rounded to the nearest thousand and therefore may not sum to totals.

[a]For the purposes of the non-CARSI allocations data, we defined regional programming as programming that benefited more than one CARSI country, or that benefited a mix of CARSI and non-CARSI countries. In those cases where the programming benefited CARSI and non-CARSI countries, we worked with agencies to determine the percentage of the overall allocated amounts that were directed to CARSI countries and updated the allocation amounts accordingly.

[b]USAID reported a negative allocation of $50,000 for regional programming for the first two quarters of fiscal year 2013, but we are reporting this number as zero.

According to State officials, the U.S. government has identified CARSI as its primary initiative for addressing citizen security threats in Central America. U.S. agencies developed an interagency strategy to ensure an integrated approach to all U.S. citizen security activities in Central America whether funded through CARSI or other sources. Established in 2012, the strategy sets up CARSI and its five goals as the national policy framework for all U.S. government citizen security efforts in Central America and states that agencies' activities in the region should link to one or more of the CARSI pillars. Agency officials noted that because the goals of CARSI are broad, a wide array of activities can be seen as supporting the goals, and agencies have sought to align their own strategy documents with the interagency strategy and five pillars of CARSI. Officials from some U.S. agencies, including DOD and the Drug Enforcement Administration (DEA), noted that the CARSI goals reflect the types of activities that their agencies were already undertaking in the region. The largest shares of non-CARSI funds allocated are from State, USAID, and DOD (see table 4).

Table 4: Estimated U.S. Non-Central America Regional Security Initiative (CARSI) Funds Allocated That Support CARSI Goals, by Agency, as of March 31, 2013

Dollars in thousands

Agency	FY 2008	FY 2009	FY 2010	FY 2011	FY 2012	FY 2013 (first two quarters)	Total
State	45,331	45,688	43,958	49,254	52,841	11,519	**248,592**
USAID	37,616	30,861	72,439	54,400	53,232	7,975	**256,523**
DOD	14,079	7,892	40,518	45,418	60,964	20,482	**189,353**
DOJ[a]	14	181	3,981	3,544	4,280	883	**12,883**
DHS	11	37	64	94	513	388	**1,107**
Non-CARSI total	**97,050**	**84,660**	**160,961**	**152,710**	**171,829**	**41,247**	**708,457**

Source: GAO analysis of DHS, DOJ, DOD, State, and USA D data.

Notes: Data are from fiscal year 2008 to the second quarter of fiscal year 2013. Non-CARSI reported amounts are from the Department of Homeland Security (DHS), Department of Justice (DOJ), Department of Defense (DOD), Department of State (State), and United States Agency for International Development (USAID). Amounts have been rounded to the nearest thousand and therefore may not sum to totals.

[a]Drug Enforcement Administration (DEA) data are not included in the DOJ totals for fiscal years 2008 and 2009 because DEA transitioned to a new financial system during fiscal year 2009 and data for these years were not readily available, according to DEA officials.

U.S. Agencies Use Non-CARSI Funding for Activities That Support CARSI Goals

U.S. agencies reported using their non-CARSI funding to implement a range of activities that supported CARSI goals, including providing training, technical assistance, equipment, infrastructure, and investigation and operational support to partner countries. For example, State funds complementary activities from a variety of non-CARSI sources, including security assistance accounts such as the International Military Education and Training account; other foreign assistance accounts, such as the Democracy Fund; and non-foreign assistance sources, such as the Conflict Stabilization Operations account. State identified 11 offices that support complementary citizen security activities in Central America with non-CARSI funds.[19] For example, according to State officials, State's Bureau of Conflict and Stabilization Operations funded mediation and community dialogue activities in Belize to reduce gang violence that complemented a related CARSI-funded activity. State's Bureau of Political-Military Affairs used non-CARSI FMF funding to provide boats to Panama's Coast Guard to assist in conducting drug interdictions in Panama's territorial waters. USAID used non-CARSI Development Assistance funds to support a variety of activities in the rule of law and human rights, good governance, political competition and conflict resolution, and education areas. For example, USAID is using non-CARSI Development Assistance funds in Guatemala to help strengthen its security and justice sector institutions, according to USAID officials.

In addition, DOD, DHS, and DOJ also use funding other than CARSI to implement activities in Central America that support CARSI goals. For example, according to officials,

- DOD has used funds from its Central Transfer Account for Counternarcotics to help establish an interagency border unit along the Guatemala/Mexico border to support Guatemalan efforts to stop the illicit movement of people and contraband. In Panama, a DOD medical team used non-CARSI funds to work with the Panamanian Ministry of Health in a poor and remote area in Panama to provide medical attention to this community. In Belize, DOD used non-CARSI funds for equipment, training, and infrastructure, including construction of a Belize Coast Guard Joint Operation Center that houses drug interdiction boats provided with funds for CARSI activities (see fig. 3).

---

[19]The 11 offices and bureaus include the Secretary's Office of Global Women's Issues and the Office to Monitor and Combat Trafficking in Persons; and the Bureaus of Political-Military Affairs; Conflict and Stabilization Operations; Democracy, Human, Rights, and Labor; Population, Refugees, and Migration; International Security and Nonproliferation; Oceans and International Environmental and Scientific Affairs; Counterterrorism; International Narcotics and Law Enforcement Affairs; and Educational and Cultural Affairs.

Figure 3: Non-Central America Regional Security Initiative Funding (CARSI) Funding for Belize Coast Guard Joint Operation Center and CARSI-Funded Equipment

Source: GAO.

- DHS and its components used non-CARSI funding to support activities such as training by Customs and Border Protection (CBP) on how to conduct searches and seizures at ports of entry that complemented other types of CARSI support.
- DOJ and its components used non-CARSI funding to support a variety of activities designed to improve partner countries' law enforcement capabilities. For example, DEA provided funding to support vetted Sensitive Investigative Units in Guatemala, Honduras, and Panama.

While not included in our reported non-CARSI allocation totals above, U.S. agencies also used other non-CARSI resources to support CARSI goals in ways other than directly funding activities in partner countries. For example, Treasury has used non-CARSI funding to pay for the salaries and other costs associated with posting its personnel in several partner countries to serve as resident advisors. These advisors work with the partner countries to improve their ability to detect and prevent money laundering and have used funding for CARSI activities to implement regional programs. In addition, the FBI's Criminal Investigations Division has not directly funded non-CARSI activities in partner countries; however, it has assigned personnel to Transnational Anti-Gang Units that have been set up in El Salvador, Guatemala, and Honduras. Agencies such as CBP, the U.S. Coast Guard, and DOD also support CARSI goals by using their assets, including aircraft and boats, to conduct counternarcotics operations in Central America. For example, U.S. agencies contribute resources to Operation Martillo, which is a joint counternarcotics operation involving the U.S. government, several partner countries, and other international partners.

State and USAID Took Steps to Consider Partner Country Needs, Absorptive Capacities, and Investments When Selecting CARSI Activities

When selecting activities to fund under CARSI, State and USAID took steps to help identify and consider partner country needs, absorptive capacities, and related U.S. and non-U.S. citizen security assistance investments in partner countries. First, State and USAID officials used assessment reports to help identify and consider partner country needs and absorptive capacities. Second, State and USAID officials used outreach meetings with officials from partner country governments, other donor governments, and international organizations to consider partner country needs, absorptive capacities, and non-U.S. citizen security assistance investments in partner countries. Third, State and USAID officials used interagency meetings at embassies in partner countries and in Washington, D.C., to coordinate U.S. efforts, as well as to help identify and consider partner country needs, absorptive capacities, and related non-U.S. investments in partner countries.

Assessment Reports Used to Help Identify and Consider Partner Country Needs and Absorptive Capacities

State officials used assessment reports to help identify and consider partner country needs and absorptive capacities when selecting activities to fund under CARSI.[20] For example, State conducted reviews of the forensic capabilities in six partner countries over the course of 2011 to evaluate the crime scene investigation, prosecution, and forensic science programs and capacities in each country. In a 2011 report, State assessed deficiencies in these areas and developed recommendations to address those deficiencies. According to State, State officials used the conclusions and recommendations from this report to inform their decisions on selecting activities to fund under CARSI. State officials also reported that they used assessment reports produced by interagency

[20]Generally, assessment reports were produced by technical subject matter experts who gathered primary data—through interviews with relevant U.S. agency and partner country officials—on any gaps or deficiencies in a partner country's capacity to provide citizen security. These reports typically include suggested solutions to address identified gaps or deficiencies.

partners to determine assistance needs, refine assistance efforts, and avoid absorptive capacity issues. For example, State officials used a series of technical assessment reports on the law enforcement and interdiction capabilities and needs of key Central American land ports of entry produced by CBP. Similarly, State officials reported that they used comprehensive assessment reports on the firearms regulations, oversight, investigative, and forensic capabilities of Central American governments produced by the Bureau of Alcohol, Tobacco, Firearms, and Explosives to determine that firearms interdiction activities could assist in reducing the trafficking of arms into the region.

USAID officials also used assessment reports to help identify and consider partner country needs and absorptive capacities when selecting activities to fund under CARSI. For example, USAID officials reported that they used assessment reports to help identify and consider partner country juvenile justice and community policing needs and absorptive capacities; these assessment reports included specific recommendations for designing and selecting juvenile justice and community policing projects in partner countries. According to USAID officials in Washington, D.C., and at U.S. embassies, USAID staff used information from these and other assessment reports to help select and design CARSI activities in partner countries. In addition, both State and USAID officials used country-specific CARSI assessment reports—produced by embassy staff in November 2009 and covering all seven partner countries—to help identify and consider partner country needs and absorptive capacities when selecting activities to fund under CARSI. These country-specific assessment reports included information on (1) the partner country's security environment, (2) embassy and host government perspectives on the effectiveness of activities implemented to date, (3) partner country strengths and weaknesses and opportunities and threats, and (4) the partner country's regional and bilateral security engagements.

Outreach Meetings Used to Help Identify and Consider Partner Country Needs, Absorptive Capacities, and Non-U.S. Investments

State and USAID officials also used outreach meetings with host government officials to help identify and consider partner country needs, absorptive capacities, and non-U.S. citizen security assistance investments in partner countries when selecting activities to fund under CARSI. Outreach meetings included both routine interactions between U.S. agency and host government officials—at the subject matter expert level—and broader, high-level meetings, typically at the ambassador and head of host government level. At these meetings, topics such as the status of current CARSI activities and the future of CARSI programming, including potential future CARSI activities, can be discussed. For example, embassy officials in one partner country reported that they held an ambassador/head of host government-level meeting with a delegation from the host government in June 2010. At this meeting, the U.S. government and the host government agreed to pursue bilateral, multiagency efforts to combat identified threats from transnational illicit trafficking and criminal organizations. Following this high-level meeting, embassy and host government officials established bilateral working groups to identify and develop activities in the partner country in areas such as border security, counternarcotics operations and strategy, gang prevention and law enforcement, community development, asset seizure, and investigation and prosecution. These bilateral working groups provided input on selecting activities to fund under CARSI and are now coordinating information-sharing efforts and progress updates on those activities.

State and USAID officials also used outreach meetings with other donor governments and international organizations to help identify and consider non-U.S. citizen security investments in partner countries when selecting CARSI activities. For example, in one partner country, embassy officials reported that they held numerous meetings with other donor governments. Through these outreach meetings, embassy officials were able to identify one donor government's investments in police intelligence in the partner country and consequently reduced funding for CARSI activities in that area. Also, through regular outreach meetings, embassy officials in the same partner country reported that they were able to identify another donor government's investments in ballistic imaging systems in the partner country. Embassy officials subsequently redirected funding for CARSI activities that would otherwise have been spent in that area.

State and USAID officials also used meetings with other donor governments through the Group of Friends of Central America's Security Experts Group to help identify and consider non-U.S. citizen security assistance investments in partner countries when selecting activities to fund under CARSI. For example, through Group of Friends and other donor meetings, State reported that they worked with another donor government to coordinate an anti-crime capacity-building activity for a partner country by de-conflicting donor purchases and leveraging investments between the U.S. and the other donor government. In addition, both USAID and State reported that they utilized a donor database on third-country and multilateral assistance hosted by the Inter-American Development Bank (IDB) to help identify and consider non-U.S. investments. The database includes information on projects sponsored by other donors and international organizations in partner countries, such as when the project started, when it is scheduled to be completed, and the total project cost. State officials said that they are eager for IDB to update the database with more detailed donor information that could increase the effectiveness of U.S. agencies' efforts to coordinate with other donors.

Interagency Meetings Used to Coordinate U.S. Efforts and Help Identify and Consider Partner Country Needs, Absorptive Capacities, and Non-U.S. Investments

When selecting activities to fund under CARSI, State and USAID officials also used interagency meetings at embassies in all seven partner countries to coordinate U.S. efforts, as well as to help identify and consider partner country needs, absorptive capacities, and related non-U.S. investments in those partner countries. For example, embassy officials in one partner country reported that they used interagency meetings to discuss the partner country's needs for a digital radio communication network to connect the host government's police, military, and related agencies and the ability of the partner country to absorb such assistance. State and DOD officials used information from the interagency meetings to help design and select a digital radio communication project using both CARSI and non-CARSI funding. According to agency officials, by involving DOD in the project selection process, embassy officials leveraged DOD's contribution to help meet the partner country's needs and help the partner country conduct joint operations with the United States. In another partner country, embassy officials reported that they used interagency meetings to identify and consider partner country needs, absorptive capacities, and related U.S. agency non-CARSI investments to support the host government's efforts to regain control over a conflict-ridden portion of the country. According to agency officials, through the interagency meetings, U.S. agencies identified and considered these factors and coordinated the use of CARSI and non-CARSI funding to support the host government's efforts.

State and USAID officials also reported that they used high-level interagency meetings, such as those of the Central America Interagency Working Group (IAWG) in Washington, D.C., to help identify and consider partner country needs and coordinate related U.S. agency non-CARSI investments in partner countries when selecting activities to fund under CARSI. The IAWG was launched in February 2012 and includes representatives from State and USAID, as well as representatives from other agencies engaged in citizen security efforts in Central America, including DHS, DOD, DOJ, and Treasury. According to State, from March 2012 through April 2013, the IAWG and its associated subgroups held 21 meetings. Through interagency meetings, State officials were able identify and consider non-CARSI proposed investments when selecting activities to fund under CARSI; for example, according to State, officials identified and considered non-CARSI proposed border management and migration projects for the region. State officials coordinated the disbursement of CARSI and non-CARSI funds to support the implementation of these border management and migration projects, while avoiding duplication among activities. In addition, through interagency meetings, agency officials were able to review various CARSI and non-CARSI land border security and interdiction activities and identified land border security short-to-medium-term capacity deficits. Consequently, agency officials are working to focus U.S. land interdiction security assistance on a limited number of high-impact engagements designed to increase seizures of contraband. By continuing to coordinate CARSI and non-CARSI investments through these interagency meetings, State officials said they will produce a more coordinated and integrated U.S. response to the region, with the goal of increasing seizures of contraband and supporting partner country border security initiatives.

U.S. Agencies Reported on Some CARSI Results, but Not on Progress toward Interagency Objectives, and Efforts Are Under Way to Evaluate CARSI Activities

Using various mechanisms, State and USAID have reported on some CARSI results at the initiative, country, and project levels. For example, embassies in partner countries produce monthly CARSI implementation reports that identify the impacts of CARSI or related activities in the country. However, U.S. agencies have not assessed or reported their performance using the metrics outlined in a 2012 interagency strategy for Central America that are designed to measure the results of CARSI and complementary non-CARSI programming.[21] USAID is currently implementing an evaluation of selected CARSI activities and State is planning an evaluation of some of its CARSI activities.

---

[21]The strategy's official title is *Central America: U.S. Citizen Security Priorities and Programs Realigning Programming and Expectations to Achieve Measurable, Sustainable and High Impact Results (2012-2017)*. This document is labeled "Sensitive But Unclassified."

U.S. Agencies Reported on Some CARSI Results through Various Mechanisms

State and USAID monitored and reported on some CARSI results through a variety of mechanisms at the initiative, country, and project levels. Initiative-level reporting addresses CARSI results across the different CARSI accounts and the seven partner countries. Country-level reporting describes CARSI results in a particular partner country. Project-level reporting describes the results of individual CARSI projects.

The Primary Source for Initiative-Level Reporting on CARSI Results Is the Annual Performance Plan and Report

According to State and USAID officials, the primary source of consolidated information on CARSI results at the initiative level—across accounts and countries—is State's Bureau of Western Hemisphere Affairs' (WHA) annual Performance Plan and Report.[22] State and USAID use the annual Performance Plan and Report to monitor the performance of foreign assistance activities in the region. In its 2012 report, WHA provides information on some CARSI-wide results using a number of performance metrics that measure outputs against WHA's established targets. For example, WHA uses metrics such as narcotics seizures and the establishment of local crime prevention groups to measure CARSI results. To produce the information on CARSI results in the report, WHA aggregated data on activities funded through all CARSI accounts and in all seven partner countries.

WHA's annual Performance Plan and Reports have identified areas where CARSI performance met or exceeded established targets, but also some areas where CARSI targets were not met. In its fiscal year 2012 report, WHA identified six CARSI-specific metrics.[23] WHA reported that CARSI results exceeded fiscal year 2012 targets for three of the six metrics. For example, for a metric related to narcotics seizures, WHA reported that the amount of seizures exceeded the established target by 62 percent. However, WHA reported that CARSI did not meet its targets for two of the six metrics. For example, CARSI results for a metric related to improvements to partner countries' court systems were 67 percent of the established target in fiscal year 2012. Finally, for the sixth CARSI-

---

[22]State and USAID require that all State and USAID offices implementing foreign assistance programs annually submit a performance plan and report that identifies the results achieved during the 12 months of the fiscal year. In addition, offices are required to set performance targets for projected results in future years. Fiscal year 2008 was the first year that offices were required to complete a performance plan and report.

[23]We do not provide more detailed information on the CARSI results discussed in the 2012 Performance Plan and Report because the document is labeled "Sensitive But Unclassified."

specific metric, State did not establish a fiscal year 2012 target against which to measure CARSI results. WHA noted that in its fiscal year 2012 report there are eight additional metrics that included combined results information on CARSI and other initiatives in the Western Hemisphere, but these metrics did not provide separate results information for CARSI-funded activities. For example, WHA reported that CARSI and other initiatives in the region together exceeded their target for a metric related to the training of foreign law enforcement officers by almost 75 percent in fiscal year 2012.

State and USAID Produce Some Country-Level Reporting on CARSI Results

State and USAID also report on CARSI results at the country level. According to State and USAID officials, monthly CARSI implementation reports produced by the embassies in each partner country are one of the key ways in which they monitor and report on CARSI results at the country level. State and USAID officials stated that these implementation reports are part of their ongoing effort to monitor the impact and effectiveness of CARSI and related non-CARSI assistance. State requires embassies to include in the reports a section discussing the impact of CARSI and related activities. These impact sections do not provide information on performance relative to established CARSI metrics or specific goals, but instead consist of descriptions of the results of various activities taking place in the partner countries over the course of the month. For example, one embassy reported in May 2013 that the host government used a body scanner purchased with CARSI funds to successfully detect a man attempting to smuggle narcotics onto a plane bound for the United States. A different embassy reported in April 2013 that a CARSI-supported anti-gang education and training program had been successfully expanded nationwide and had taught over 3,000 children over 3 years of the program. The 55 monthly reports we reviewed included a range of other results from CARSI-funded activities that were identified by embassies, but we also found that some embassies did not always link some of the reported results to specific U.S. assistance activities.[24] For example, a number of reports noted seizures or arrests made by the host government, but the reports did not provide any information on how CARSI or related U.S. non-CARSI assistance had facilitated these efforts.

---

[24]We reviewed 8 reports from each of the seven partner countries except Nicaragua, for which we reviewed 7 reports, for a total of 55 reports. We asked State to provide the 3 most recent reports produced by each embassy as of May 2013, as well as reports from earlier years going back to fiscal year 2009.

State officials identified INL's annual end-use monitoring reports as a second mechanism for monitoring and reporting on CARSI activities at the country level, although these end-use monitoring reports are not specific to CARSI. State officials said that these end-use monitoring reports are used to monitor all INCLE-funded items that have been provided to the partner country to ensure that items are accounted for and used in accordance with the terms agreed to by the U.S. government and the partner country.[25] As part of the end-use monitoring reports, State requires embassy officials to include a discussion of the impact of any INCLE-funded equipment, infrastructure, training, or other services that have been provided, including under CARSI. The reports from partner countries for fiscal years 2009 through 2012 identified a number of positive results from CARSI assistance. For example, the embassy in El Salvador stated in its 2012 end-use monitoring report that trucks provided to the national police had a significant impact on the number of cases investigated and improved the national police's response capabilities. However, the reports also identified some issues related to upkeep, maintenance, and use of CARSI-funded equipment. For example, the embassy in Guatemala reported in 2012 that 11 motorcycles provided to the National Police became inoperable as a result of a lack of proper maintenance and funding; State then covered the cost of refurbishing the motorcycles.

Finally, USAID officials noted that annual portfolio reviews conducted by USAID missions in partner countries are an important tool for reporting CARSI results at the country level. USAID first began requiring its missions to conduct such reviews in November 2012. According to USAID guidance, portfolio reviews should, among other things, examine the mission's progress in achieving its objectives over the past year. The portfolio reviews that we examined included varying levels of information about CARSI results. For example, one review did not provide any results information, but instead provided a general description of the types of

---

[25]Federal law requires that all reasonable steps are taken to ensure that aircraft and other equipment made available to foreign countries by INL are used only in ways that are consistent with the purposes for which such equipment was made available (22 U.S.C. sec. 2291c(b)). In addition, federal law requires the establishment of a program to monitor the end use of all defense articles and services sold, leased, or exported under the Arms Export Control Act or the Foreign Assistance Act of 1961, as amended, in order to provide reasonable assurance that the recipient is complying with requirements imposed by the U.S. government and that such articles and services are being used for the purposes for which they are provided. 22 U.S.C. § 2785.

activities funded under the USAID mission's portfolio. However, in other cases, the USAID missions did provide specific results information. For example, one mission reported that one of its programs had provided access to vocational training to improve job competitiveness for 1,763 young people either at risk of becoming gang members or trying to leave gangs. In some cases, the portfolio reviews did not specify whether certain results were from CARSI or related non-CARSI projects.

State and USAID Perform Some Project-Level Reporting That Identifies the Results of Individual CARSI Projects

State and USAID officials also stated that they perform certain monitoring and reporting on CARSI results at the project level. State's INL conducts quarterly desk reviews of INCLE-funded CARSI activities to track the progress of projects over time. INL requires these quarterly desk reviews to include a discussion of the project objectives, measure project results against established performance metrics, and identify success stories. For example, INL reported in the quarterly desk review for one CARSI project that, as of the end of 2012, it had trained 259 host government investigators, prosecutors, and judges on the use of forensic evidence in court proceedings. In another quarterly desk review, INL reported that the project implementer had successfully developed an improved case management system to assist the Costa Rican Attorney General's Office in conducting drug trafficking prosecutions. USAID also conducts quarterly reporting on its CARSI projects. USAID's quarterly reports include information on the project's accomplishments for the quarter and progress that had been made relative to the project's established performance metrics. For example, in a report for the second quarter of fiscal year 2013, the implementer of USAID's crime prevention program in Panama reported that it had met or exceeded its targets for 20 of the project's 26 metrics, including its target for the number of municipalities that had set up municipal crime prevention committees.

U.S. Agencies Have Not Assessed and Reported Progress toward Objectives Outlined in the U.S. Interagency Strategy for Central America

While State and USAID have reported on some CARSI results, U.S. agencies have not assessed and reported on their results using the performance metrics identified in the February 2012 interagency citizen security strategy for Central America. U.S. agencies developed this strategy to help coordinate and focus the U.S. government's CARSI and related non-CARSI activities in the region. In the interagency strategy, U.S. agencies outlined five metrics for measuring the performance of U.S. government citizen security programming, including CARSI activities, in achieving the strategy's objectives. For example, the strategy includes a metric to reduce homicide rates each year from 2012 through 2017.[26] According to State and USAID officials, the strategy and the metrics it identifies were developed through an iterative, interagency process that included other agencies such as DOD, DOJ, and DHS. However, to date, U.S. agencies have not assessed and reported on their performance using the metrics identified in the strategy.

According to WHA officials, the Central America Interagency Working Group plans to discuss how the U.S. government should report out on the strategy's metrics, but also noted some challenges that agencies could face in doing so. For example, officials said that it may be difficult for U.S. agencies to separate out and delineate the impact of U.S. agencies' activities from the impact of partner country activities independently conducted without U.S. assistance. Officials also noted that it is challenging to assess progress using some of the metrics, such as a metric addressing reductions in impunity rates in selected communities, because the necessary data may not be readily available. We recognize that collecting performance data may be challenging and could require some adjustments to performance metrics. However, in our 2012 report that identified key considerations for successfully implementing interagency collaboration mechanisms, such as the interagency strategy for Central America, we found that a key feature in the successful implementation of such mechanisms is the development of a system for monitoring and reporting on results.[27] Such a system is important because it helps the agencies involved in the interagency effort identify areas for improvement. In addition, in our past work identifying leading practices for performance management, we concluded that collecting performance data is a critical practice for agencies because it provides agencies with crucial information to guide decision making.[28] Without assessing progress in achieving the objectives in the interagency strategy, U.S. agencies lack important information on the performance of CARSI and related activities that could help guide future decision making. Such information is important because, as noted in the strategy, the U.S. government is seeking to support a small number of high-impact activities

---

[26]We do not provide more detailed descriptions of the strategy's metrics because the strategy is labeled "Sensitive But Unclassified."

[27]GAO-12-1022.

[28]GAO/GGD-96-118.

that have proven their effectiveness in solving the region's most pressing problems.

USAID Is Conducting an Evaluation of Some of Its CARSI Activities, and State Is Planning an Evaluation

USAID is currently conducting an evaluation of some of its CARSI activities, and State is developing an evaluation of INL activities under CARSI, consistent with its evaluation policy. USAID and State have both taken steps to monitor and report on the results of CARSI-funded activities. However, in our previous work we concluded that monitoring activities do not take the place of program evaluations.[29] As we previously concluded, monitoring is ongoing in nature and measures agencies' progress in meeting established objectives, typically using performance metrics. Evaluations are individual, systematic studies that typically examine a broader range of information on program performance and its context than is feasible to monitor on an ongoing basis. Thus, evaluations allow for overall assessments of whether a program is working and what adjustments need to be made to improve results.

USAID is overseeing an impact evaluation to be completed in 2014 of its CARSI municipal crime prevention programming, which is the largest of its three major programming areas under CARSI.[30] The evaluation, which is being conducted by Vanderbilt University on behalf of USAID, is examining the impact of the program in El Salvador, Guatemala, Honduras, and Panama. For the study, Vanderbilt randomly assigned more than 100 neighborhoods to treatment and control groups, with the treatment neighborhoods receiving assistance under the program. To measure the impact of the program over time, Vanderbilt is collecting baseline, midpoint, and final data from the communities using both quantitative and qualitative data collection tools. As of July 2013, Vanderbilt was in the process of gathering and analyzing the midpoint data for the evaluation. According to USAID officials, the midpoint findings are still tentative and subject to change, but the preliminary results suggest that the programming has been effective in improving security in the targeted communities. For example, USAID officials stated that the

---

[29]GAO, *Performance Measurement and Evaluation: Definitions and Relationships,* GAO-11-646SP (Washington, D.C.: May 2011).

[30]USAID officials stated that they will also conduct evaluations of other CARSI activities that meet the criteria established in USAID's 2011 evaluation policy. USAID's evaluation policy requires each USAID operating unit to evaluate all projects that equal or exceed the average project size for that operating unit, at least once during the project's lifetime.

preliminary results from El Salvador show that murder and robbery rates have been reduced in communities receiving USAID assistance under the program.

USAID officials identified a range of ways that they expect the crime prevention programming evaluation to assist them, once it is completed. For example, they expect the evaluation to provide evidence of the extent to which USAID's crime prevention program reduced crime victimization and perceptions of insecurity in at-risk communities. USAID officials also anticipated that they would be able to use the evaluation's findings as a tool to encourage partner countries to make their own investments in crime prevention activities.

State officials noted that they are currently working on a scope of work for an evaluation of CARSI activities. In 2012, State issued an evaluation policy that requires bureaus to evaluate two to four programs, projects, or activities every 2 years, starting in fiscal year 2012, with all "large" programs, projects, and activities required to be evaluated at least once in their lifetime or every 5 years, whichever is less.[31] The policy also requires all State bureaus to complete a bureau evaluation plan and to update it annually. According to State officials, given other priority areas, INL did not select CARSI for evaluation in its first bureau evaluation plan, covering fiscal years 2012 through 2014, although CARSI qualifies as a large program for INL. Nevertheless, INL officials stated that they intend to conduct an evaluation of their CARSI activities beginning in fiscal year 2014, as CARSI approaches its 5-year point. INL officials stated that they are currently working on a scope of work for this evaluation, which will cover CARSI programming across the partner countries. INL officials stated that their intention is to issue a solicitation by the end of 2013 for a contractor to conduct the CARSI evaluation. However, INL officials noted that many decisions have not yet been made about the scope or methodology for the evaluation and that funding has not yet been secured for the evaluation. In regard to WHA, State officials noted that the bureau manages only a small percentage of State's funding for CARSI activities. Given the small percentage of CARSI funding WHA manages, State

---

[31]See State, *Department of State Program Evaluation Policy* (Washington, D.C.: Feb. 23, 2012). The policy states that for each bureau, a "large" program, project, or activity is one where the dollar value or number of staff resources used is equal to or greater than the median amount for the bureau.

officials said that WHA does not have any plans to conduct a separate CARSI evaluation from the one INL intends to do.

Our guidance on evaluation design indicates that State could increase the value of any future evaluation it conducts by ensuring that it systematically plans the evaluation. As we have previously concluded, systematically planning for evaluations is important to (1) enhance the quality, credibility, and usefulness of evaluations and (2) use time and resources effectively.[32] In our earlier work on evaluation design, we recommended that agencies take five steps to effectively design an evaluation, as shown in table 5.

Table 5: GAO-Recommended Steps for Evaluation Design	
1	Clarify understanding of the program's goals and strategy.
2	Develop relevant and useful evaluation questions.
3	Select an appropriate evaluation approach or design for each evaluation question.
4	Identify data sources and collection procedures to obtain relevant, credible information.
5	Develop plans to analyze the data in ways that allow valid conclusions to be drawn from the evaluation questions.

Source: GAO.

Evaluations of CARSI activities, such as the one that INL has stated it intends to undertake, could provide State with important information to help it manage and oversee CARSI. As State's evaluation policy notes, evaluations are essential to documenting program impact and identifying best practices and lessons learned. Among other things, an evaluation could help State as it seeks to identify successful CARSI activities and determine how best to replicate them in other locations.

State officials noted that designing a CARSI evaluation will be challenging because CARSI involves a diverse set of activities that are being implemented in seven different countries. Thus, State officials stated that one challenge they will face in evaluating CARSI is selecting a mix of activities to evaluate that are sufficiently representative of their various CARSI activities that conclusions can be drawn about the broader impact

[32]GAO, *Designing Evaluations: 2012 Revision*, GAO-12-208G (Washington, D.C.: Jan. 2012).

of their CARSI efforts. Given such challenges, effectively planning any CARSI evaluation would help State ensure that the evaluation provides the types of information it can use to guide future decisions about CARSI programming.

Conclusions

CARSI partner countries face significant challenges that threaten the security of their citizens as well as the interests of the United States. U.S. agencies have allocated over $1.2 billion to support a range of activities to help partner countries respond to these threats. While State and USAID have reported on some results from CARSI-funded activities, the agencies have not worked with their interagency partners to assess progress made in meeting performance targets outlined in the 2012 U.S. interagency citizen security strategy for Central America. Without assessing their performance meeting these targets, agencies lack important information on progress made toward achieving the objectives outlined in the interagency strategy that could help guide future decisions. To evaluate some of its CARSI activities, USAID is currently overseeing an evaluation of its CARSI crime prevention programming and intends to use the evaluation to help it better target, design, and prioritize future CARSI programming. State is planning an evaluation of some of its CARSI activities as the initiative approaches its 5-year mark. These evaluations will help agencies better manage and oversee their programs and activities. Among other things, the evaluations can be used to (1) help agencies assess the effectiveness of completed activities, (2) modify the current mix of existing projects to increase program effectiveness, and (3) better prioritize future projects to achieve results. While these are commendable steps, assessing progress made toward achieving the objectives outlined in the U.S. interagency strategy for Central America would provide important information on the performance of CARSI and related U.S. government activities and better guide U.S. decision making.

Recommendation for Executive Action

To help ensure that U.S. agencies have relevant information on the progress of CARSI and related U.S. government activities, we recommend that the Secretary of State and the USAID Administrator direct their representatives on the Central America Interagency Working Group to work with the other members to assess the progress of CARSI and related U.S. government activities in achieving the objectives outlined in the U.S. government's interagency citizen security strategy for Central America.

Agency Comments and Our Evaluation

We provided a draft of this report to DHS, DOD, DOJ, State, Treasury, and USAID for their review and comment. DHS, State, and USAID provided technical comments, which we incorporated as appropriate. USAID and State also provided written comments, which are reproduced in appendixes IV and V, respectively. In their written comments, State and USAID both concurred with our recommendation and State noted that GAO's recommended steps for evaluation design would guide an evaluation of CARSI programming.

As discussed with your offices, unless you publicly announce the contents of this report earlier, we plan no further distribution until 30 days from the report date. At that time, we will send copies to DHS, DOD, DOJ, State, Treasury, and USAID, and other interested parties. In addition, the report will be available at no charge on GAO's website at http://www.gao.gov.

If you or your staff have any questions about this report, please contact me at (202) 512-7331 or johnsoncm@gao.gov. Contact points for our Offices of Congressional Relations and Public Affairs may be found on the last page of this report. GAO staff who made key contributions to this report are listed in appendix VI.

Charles Michael Johnson, Jr.
Director
International Affairs and Trade

Appendix I: Scope and Methodology

This report (1) provides an updated assessment of U.S. agencies' funding and activities that support Central America Regional Security Initiative (CARSI) goals; (2) examines whether U.S. agencies took steps to consider partner country needs, absorptive capacities, and related U.S. and non-U.S. investments when selecting activities to fund under CARSI; and (3) examines information on the extent to which U.S. agencies reported CARSI results and evaluated CARSI activities.

To assess U.S. agencies' funding and activities that supported CARSI goals, we obtained data and program documentation from the Department of State (State) and the United States Agency for International Development (USAID) concerning funds allocated to support programs in Central American countries under the Mérida Initiative in fiscal years 2008 and 2009 and under CARSI from fiscal year 2010 to June 1, 2013, through four accounts—International Narcotics Control and Law Enforcement (INCLE); Economic Support Fund (ESF); Nonproliferation, Anti-terrorism, Demining, and Related Programs (NADR); and Foreign Military Financing (FMF). We obtained the data from each bureau at State that administers those accounts: International Narcotics and Law Enforcement Affairs (INL), Western Hemisphere Affairs (WHA), International Security and Nonproliferation, Counterterrorism, and Political-Military Affairs. We also obtained data from USAID, which also allocates and implements the ESF account. In particular, State and USAID provided data on the status of allocations, unobligated balances, unliquidated obligations, and disbursements for the ESF account; State also provided these data for the INCLE and NADR accounts. State's bureaus and USAID administer the accounts separately and utilize their own data collection systems and budgeting terms.

To address differences between their systems, we provided State and USAID with the definitions from GAO's *A Glossary of Terms Used in the Federal Budget Process* and requested that State and USAID provide the relevant data according to those definitions.[1] To the extent possible, we worked with agencies to ensure that they provided data that met these definitions. However, the Department of Defense budgets and tracks FMF funds in a different way than the other foreign assistance accounts that support CARSI. The Defense Security Cooperation Agency (DSCA) and

---

[1]GAO, *A Glossary of Terms Used in the Federal Budget Process*, GAO-05-734SP (Washington, D.C.: Sept. 2005).

the Defense Financing and Accounting Service (DFAS) are responsible for the financial systems that account for FMF funds, as well as tracking the implementation and disbursement of those funds. DSCA's system can only track FMF uncommitted and committed amounts, not unliquidated obligations or disbursements. DFAS tracks disbursements using the Defense Integrated Finance System; however, there is no direct link between the DSCA and DFAS systems and the DFAS system does not track funding for specific initiatives, such as CARSI. Therefore, State was not able to provide data on unliquidated obligations or disbursements, but it was able to provide us with data on CARSI FMF allocations and commitments.

In providing technical comments on a draft of this report, State officials reported an amount of close to $10.6 million in additional INCLE funding that was allocated for CARSI activities in fiscal year 2010 that had not been previously reported to GAO. State officials also said that they could not provide obligation or disbursement information related to this amount because these INCLE funds are centrally managed and State's financial systems do not allow them to track such funds by region or country. According to State, that is why these funds were not previously reported to GAO. We followed up with State officials to confirm that the funds had been applied to CARSI activities and to document the programs toward which the funds had been applied. Although State officials were not able to provide information for the obligation or disbursement of these funds, we have included this amount in the total allocated for CARSI activities. We made note of this discrepancy in presenting this data in the report.[2]

We also interviewed officials from each of State's bureaus and USAID on their budgeting process and terms to determine the best method for collecting comparable data across accounts. We then reviewed the data and consulted with State and USAID on the accuracy and completeness of the information. When we found discrepancies, we contacted relevant agency officials and worked with them to resolve the discrepancies. We noted any differences in the ways the agencies collected, categorized, or reported their data in notes to the tables in this report. To assess the reliability of the data provided, we requested and reviewed information from agency officials regarding the underlying financial data systems and

---

[2]Because State was unable provide a breakout of this almost $10.6 million in INCLE funds, total allocations of $484 million, which excludes this amount, were used to make comparisons against obligations and disbursements.

the checks, controls, and reviews used to generate the data and ensure its accuracy and reliability. We determined that the data provided were sufficiently reliable for the purposes of this report. Furthermore, to identify equipment, training, and other related activities supported by funding for CARSI activities, we reviewed program documentation and interviewed relevant officials from State and USAID regarding the status of program implementation and the types of equipment, training, and other activities provided to partner countries to date. In addition, we visited three partner countries—Belize, Guatemala, and Panama. We selected these three countries as a sample considering the following elements—the scope of the citizen security problem; the amount of funding for CARSI activities received from fiscal years 2008 to 2012, the range of CARSI activities undertaken, the extent of non-CARSI U.S. government activities that support CARSI objectives, and the extent of host government or other donor citizen security efforts in these countries. In these three countries, we met with U.S. agency officials as well as host government, international organization, and other donor government officials. We also visited CARSI and non-CARSI activity locations during these visits.

To determine how much non-CARSI assistance has been allocated for partner countries that supported CARSI goals, we collected data from State and USAID as well as DOD, the Department of Justice, the Department of Homeland Security, and the Department of the Treasury for fiscal year 2008 through the second quarter of fiscal year 2013. Data on disbursements of non-CARSI funding were not readily available for some agencies because of the complexity and challenges associated with how these agencies track their disbursement data. In collecting allocation data, we asked agencies to provide funding data only for activities that they determined supported one or more of the five pillars of CARSI. In addition, we asked agencies to provide only data on non-CARSI funding that directly assisted partner countries, such as funding for training, equipment, infrastructure, and operational or investigative support. To avoid double-counting across agencies, we asked agencies to provide data only on activities funded through their own appropriations. We requested non-CARSI data from all the agencies in a standardized format, but given differences in the agencies' missions, budget processes, and data systems, there were variations in the responses we received. We worked with the agencies to resolve these discrepancies. For example, some agencies provided data on funding for the salaries of U.S. government employees, or the operation of U.S. equipment, such as aircraft. We determined that these types of funding did not constitute direct assistance to the partner countries and did not include these funding amounts in our totals. In addition, in certain cases, agencies reported that they did not allocate non-CARSI funding to activities supporting CARSI goals in advance, but that they disbursed resources to programs that supported CARSI goals as needs arose. In these cases, we worked with the agencies to determine whether or not the disbursed amounts could be considered as equivalent to the allocation amounts given the nature of how the agencies' programming was executed and made adjustments accordingly.

To assess the reliability of the non-CARSI data provided, we collected information from agency officials regarding their methodology for determining what non-CARSI funding to include as supporting CARSI goals and the process they used for generating the data. We worked with agencies to make adjustments to these methodologies if we identified concerns. As part of this effort, we gathered information from the agencies on potential risks of underestimates or overestimates of the allocation amounts they reported and how we might mitigate any potential overestimates. We then took steps to mitigate these issues to the extent possible. For example, some agencies provided us with funding data for regional programs that benefited both partner countries and non-CARSI countries. In these cases, we worked with the agencies to determine if there was an appropriate way of apportioning a percentage of the costs to the partner countries versus the other non-CARSI beneficiary countries. If possible, we adjusted the numbers accordingly; if adjustments were not feasible, we did not include the funding amounts in our totals. As part of our data reliability assessments, we also reviewed information on the underlying data systems used to produce the data and the checks, controls, and reviews the agencies perform to ensure the accuracy and reliability of data in these systems. There are certain inherent limitations in the data we collected because agencies were asked to make determinations, using their own judgments, about what portions of their non-CARSI funding supported CARSI goals. However, we believe that the steps we have taken mitigate these limitations, to the extent possible. Given this, we determined that, for the purposes of this report, the data were sufficiently reliable to provide estimates of agencies' non-CARSI funding that supported CARSI goals. To determine the types of activities that this non-CARSI assistance funded, we reviewed documentation from U.S. agencies and also conducted interviews with agency officials at headquarters and in our three site-visit countries.

To examine whether U.S. agencies took steps to consider partner country needs, absorptive capacities, and related U.S. and non-U.S. investments when selecting activities to fund under CARSI, we interviewed State and USAID officials at headquarters and at the embassies in the three partner countries we visited. In addition, we submitted specific written questions to two bureaus at State and USAID at headquarters and received written response documents on the steps State and USAID officials used to help identify and consider these key factors when selecting activities for funding under CARSI. We also worked with State officials at headquarters to develop written questions for the embassies in all seven partner countries on the steps they used to help identify and consider these key factors when selecting CARSI activities. We received comprehensive written response documents from the embassies in all partner countries with information cleared at the Deputy Chief of Mission level. We reviewed and analyzed the written response documents we received from two bureaus at State and USAID at headquarters and from embassies in all seven partner countries. Using these various data sources, we identified specific steps that State and USAID officials used to consider partner country needs, absorptive capacities, and investments when selecting CARSI activities. We also reviewed additional available written documentation on the steps State and USAID used to help identify and consider key factors, such as various assessment reports produced by State, USAID, and other agency officials; trip reports and status reports produced by agency officials; summary agendas from interagency meetings held at embassies and in headquarters; and documentation on the management and coordination of CARSI activities. We did not assess the extent or effectiveness of the steps that State and USAID took to identify and consider partner country needs, absorptive capacities, or U.S. and non-U.S. investments.

To examine information on the extent to which U.S. agencies reported CARSI results and evaluated CARSI activities, we interviewed State and USAID officials at headquarters and U.S. officials at the embassies in the three partner countries we visited. In addition, we submitted questions and received written responses from State and USAID headquarters, as well as from the embassies in all seven partner countries, which provided additional information on agencies' results reporting and evaluation of CARSI activities. Using this information, we identified the key mechanisms State and USAID use for reporting CARSI results at the program, country, and project level. At the initiative level, we reviewed the WHA annual Performance Plan and Reports for fiscal years 2009 through 2012 and the interagency strategy for citizen security in Central America and assessed the types of CARSI results identified in these documents. At the country level, we analyzed a non-probability sample of 55 monthly CARSI implementation reports produced by embassies in the partner countries. We selected this sample to ensure that we obtained a mix of old and recent reports from all 7 countries. This sample contained eight reports from each of the seven partner countries, except for Nicaragua, which provided seven reports, and included the three most recent reports produced by each embassy as of May 2013, as well as reports from earlier years going back to fiscal year 2009. At the country level, we also reviewed completed INL annual End-Use Monitoring Reports from each of the seven partner countries for fiscal years 2009 to 2012 and a USAID-selected sample of five portfolio reviews from USAID offices in partner countries.[3] Finally, we analyzed five INL Quarterly Desk Reviews and six USAID project reports to determine the types of CARSI results identified in project-level reporting. These reports were selected by State and USAID respectively as examples of their project-level reporting.

We also compared U.S. agencies' actions to assess and report their progress toward achieving the objectives in the interagency strategy for Central America against key considerations that we identified in 2012 for implementing interagency collaboration mechanisms.[4] In our previous work, we found that one key feature in the successful implementation of such mechanisms is the development of a system for monitoring and reporting on results. In addition, we compared agencies' activities against leading practices we identified in 1996 for performance management of federal programs.[5]

Given the wide variety of reporting done by State and USAID that identifies CARSI results, we were not able to provide comprehensive information on CARSI results. The results identified in the report are meant only as illustrative examples of the types of results identified by State and USAID and are not generalizable. We also used the interviews with State and USAID officials to determine the status of any completed,

---

[3]The embassy in Nicaragua did not complete End-Use Monitoring Reports for fiscal years 2009 and 2010. The six other embassies completed End-Use Monitoring Reports for all four fiscal years.

[4]We developed this list of considerations through a review of relevant literature on collaboration mechanisms, interviews with experts on collaboration, and a review of findings from a number of our previous reports on collaboration in the federal government. See GAO, *Managing for Results: Key Considerations for Implementing Interagency Collaborative Mechanisms*, GAO-12-1022 (Washington, D.C.: Sept. 27, 2012).

[5]We developed this list of practices through the study of the experiences of leading public sector organizations, a review of management studies of federal agencies, and interviews with federal executives and other experts on performance management. See GAO, *Executive Guide: Effectively Implementing the Government Performance and Results Act,* GAO/GGD-96-118 (Washington, D.C.: June 1996).

ongoing, or planned evaluations of CARSI. From USAID, we gathered information on the scope and methodology, current status, and expected uses of their impact evaluation of their municipal crime prevention program. We also gathered testimonial evidence from State on INL's planned evaluation of its CARSI activities. In addition, we reviewed State's 2012 Program Evaluation Policy and determined the extent to which INL and WHA had selected CARSI activities for evaluation in their bureau evaluation plans for fiscal years 2012 through 2014.

We conducted this performance audit from August 2012 to September 2013 in accordance with generally accepted government auditing standards. Those standards require that we plan and perform the audit to obtain sufficient, appropriate evidence to provide a reasonable basis for our findings and conclusions based on our audit objectives. We believe that the evidence obtained provides a reasonable basis for our findings and conclusions based on our audit objectives.

Appendix II: Status of Central America Regional Security Initiative Funds

To demonstrate how funding for Central America Regional Security Initiative (CARSI) activities have been allocated, obligated, and disbursed, we are providing the status of funds provided for CARSI activities as of June 1, 2013. The following tables show CARSI funds by account, describing how U.S. agencies have allocated, obligated, and disbursed funds (by year of appropriation) toward activities in partner countries. In addition, the tables show unobligated balances, which is the portion of an obligational authority that has not yet been obligated, and unliquidated obligations (or obligated balance), which is the amount of obligation already incurred for which payment has not yet been made.[1] Funding for CARSI activities has primarily come from the International Narcotics Control and Law Enforcement (INCLE) and Economic Support Fund (ESF) accounts. In earlier years, funding also came from the Nonproliferation, Anti-terrorism, Demining, and Related Programs (NADR) and Foreign Military Financing (FMF) accounts.

Status of CARSI INCLE Account Funds

The Department of State's (State) Bureau for International Narcotics and Law Enforcement Affairs administers the CARSI INCLE funds. As of June 1, 2013, State had allocated the largest amount of its CARSI INCLE funds to Guatemala, regional programs, Honduras, and El Salvador (see table 6). In addition, State had disbursed approximately $122 million of INCLE funds to support partner countries (see table 7). In providing technical comments on a draft of this report, State officials reported an amount of close to $10.6 million in INCLE funding that was allocated for CARSI activities in fiscal year 2010 that had not been previously reported to GAO. State officials also said that they could not provide obligation or disbursement information related to this amount, because these INCLE funds are centrally managed and State's financial systems do not allow them to track such funds by region or country. According to State, this is why these funds were not previously reported to GAO. We followed up with State officials to confirm that the funds had been applied to CARSI activities and to document the programs toward which the funds had been applied. Although State officials were not able to provide information on the obligation or disbursement of these funds, we have included this amount in the INCLE funding allocated for CARSI activities.

---

[1]GAO, *A Glossary of Terms Used in the Federal Budget Process*, GAO-05-734SP (Washington, D.C.: Sept. 2005).

Table 6: International Narcotics Control and Law Enforcement (INCLE) Funding Allocated and Disbursed, by Fiscal Year Appropriated, toward Central America Regional Security Initiative (CARSI) Activities in Partner Countries, as of June 1, 2013

Dollars in thousands

Country	FY2008	FY2009	FY2010	FY2011[a]	FY2012	FY2013[b]	Total
Belize							
Allocated	1,152	2,569[c]	3,388[c]	3,067	3,725	0	13,901
Unobligated balance	0	0	2[d]	6[d]	0	0	8
Unliquidated obligations	4	793	2,657	2,477	3,499	0	9,430
Disbursed[e]	1,148	1,776	730	584	226	0	4,464
Costa Rica							
Allocated	2,118	5,120	3,295	7,782[c]	5,919	0	24,234
Unobligated balance	0	0[d,f]	1[f]	0	0	0	1
Unliquidated obligations	453	2,370	1,579	6,510	5,718	0	16,630
Disbursed[e]	1,665	2,750	1,715	1,272	201	0	7,603
Costa Rica Bilateral							
Allocated	0	0	500	0	0	0	500
Unobligated balance	0	0	0	0	0	0	0
Unliquidated obligations	0	0	0	0	0	0	0
Disbursed[e]	0	0	500	0	0	0	500
El Salvador							
Allocated	4,452	12,781[c]	5,359[c]	9,344	9,106	0	41,042
Unobligated balance	0	1[f]	1[d]	0	0	0	2
Unliquidated obligations	743	3,957	3,444	8,071	8,447	0	24,662
Disbursed[e]	3,709	8,823	1,913	1,273	659	0	16,377
Guatemala							
Allocated	5,464	12,109	19,272	20,812	16,839	0	74,496
Unobligated balance	0	2[d]	2[d]	0	0	0	4
Unliquidated obligations	439	4,658	7,503	16,914	15,508	0	45,022
Disbursed[e]	5,025	7,450	11,767	3,899	1,331	0	29,472
Guatemala Bilateral							
Allocated	0	0	1,500	0	0	0	1,500
Unobligated balance	0	0	0	0	0	0	0
Unliquidated obligations	0	0	532	0	0	0	532
Disbursed[e]	0	0	968	0	0	0	968
Honduras							
Allocated	4,469	5,571	6,585	13,201	17,613	0	47,439

Dollars in thousands

Country	FY2008	FY2009	FY2010	FY2011[a]	FY2012	FY2013[b]	Total
Unobligated balance	0	0	0	0	0	0	0
Unliquidated obligations	811	1,119	3,733	9,111	17,125	0	31,899
Disbursed[e]	3,658	4,452	2,852	4,089	488	0	15,539
Nicaragua							
Allocated	1,431	3,045	1,192	971	369	0	7,008
Unobligated balance	0	400[d]	8[d]	0[d]	0	0	408
Unliquidated obligations	715	1,607	655	780	287	0	4,044
Disbursed[e]	716	1,038	529	190	81	0	2,554
Panama							
Allocated	2,097	10,782	5,186	10,297[c]	9,663	0	38,025
Unobligated balance	0	0	0	0	0	0	0
Unliquidated obligations	295	2,709	1,217	6,791	8,576	0	19,588
Disbursed[e]	1,802	8,073	3,969	3,505	1,087	0	18,436
Regional[g]							
Allocated	3,752	18,023	8,135	6,033	21,766	0	57,709
Unobligated balance	0	0	0	0	10,586[d]	0	10,586
Unliquidated obligations	1,057	2,930	4,603	2,909	9,446	0	20,945
Disbursed[e]	2,695	15,093	3,532	3,124	1,735	0	26,179
INCLE Centrally Managed Account[h]							
Allocated	--	--	10,588	--	--	--	10,588
Unobligated balance	--	--	N/A	--	--	--	N/A
Unliquidated obligations	--	--	N/A	--	--	--	N/A
Disbursed	--	--	N/A	--	--	--	N/A

Source: GAO analysis of State data.

Notes: Amounts have been rounded to the nearest thousand and therefore may not sum to totals. In the Bureau of International Narcotics and Law Enforcement Affairs financial tracking database, disbursed amounts are labeled as dispensed amounts and allocated amounts are labeled as values allocated. State has 5 years from the time that the period of availability for obligation expires to disburse INCLE funds.

[a]Fiscal year 2011 allocated amounts differ from the amounts we reported in GAO-13-295R because we reported amounts as of September 30, 2011. Regional funds were further allocated for CARSI partner countries in fiscal year 2012, increasing the allocated amounts for individual CARSI countries and decreasing the regional allocated amount.

[b]Data cover 8 months of fiscal year 2013, from October 1, 2012, through June 1, 2013.

[c]For the purposes of this report, "allocated" amounts include funds for vetted units in these countries. The funding for the vetted units is tracked in the year in which the funds were allocated.

[d]According to State officials, unobligated balances from fiscal years 2008, 2009, 2010, and 2011 are no longer available for obligation. Unobligated balances from fiscal year 2012 are available for obligation until September 30, 2013. Unobligated balances from fiscal year 2013 are available for obligations until September 30, 2014.

eAccording to State officials, payments applied to an obligation in the accounting system are recorded as disbursements or liquidations for INCLE.

fBecause we are presenting budget data in thousands of dollars, amounts under $1,000 are reported as zero. For Costa Rica the amount is $288 and $626; for El Salvador the amount is $858; for Nicaragua the amount is $353 and $126; for Panama the amount is $23; and for Regional the amount is $350.

g"Regional" refers to funding for CARSI region-wide programs in Central America that is not tied to a program in a specific country.

hState was only able to provide allocated amounts for CARSI activities from this account. According to State officials, these INCLE funds are centrally managed and are not tracked by region or country; therefore, State was not able to provide information on the unobligated balance, unliquidated obligations, and disbursements of these funds. N/A indicates that these data are not available. Dashes indicate "not applicable".

Table 7: International Narcotics Control and Law Enforcement (INCLE) Funding, by Fiscal Year, in Current Dollars, to Support Central America Regional Security Initiative (CARSI) Activities as of June 1, 2013

Dollars in thousands

Country	2008	2009	2010	2011	2012	2013[a]	Total
Belize	0	13	746	675	2,194	836	4,463
Costa Rica	0	1	768	1,861	1,196	3,778	7,604
Costa Rica Bilateral	0	0	0	21	101	378	500
El Salvador	0	353	1,482	4,092	6,117	4,333	16,377
Guatemala	0	1,001	1,630	6,258	15,725	4,858	29,472
Guatemala Bilateral	0	0	0	469	481	19	969
Honduras	0	0	100	3,596	6,198	5,644	15,538
Nicaragua	0	23	157	901	1,374	99	2,554
Panama	0	267	2,813	4,773	5,861	4,723	18,437
Regional	0	35	9,306	3,032	8,476	5,331	26,180
INCLE Centrally Managed Account[b]	--	--	N/A	N/A	N/A	N/A	N/A
CARSI INCLE total	0	1,693	17,002	25,678	47,723	29,999	122,094

Source: GAO analysis of State data.

Notes: Amounts have been rounded to the nearest thousand and therefore may not sum to totals.

aData cover 8 months of fiscal year 2013, from October 1, 2012, through June 1, 2013.

bAccording to State officials, these INCLE funds are centrally managed and are not tracked by region or country; therefore, State was not able to provide information on the disbursements of these funds. N/A indicates that these data are not available. Dashes indicate "not applicable".

Status of CARSI ESF Account Funds

The United States Agency for International Development (USAID) shares responsibility with State to administer the ESF account. USAID oversees the implementation of most programs funded from this account, according to USAID officials; State's Bureau for Western Hemisphere Affairs administers State's portion of ESF.

Status of USAID's ESF Funding for CARSI Activities

As of June 1, 2013, USAID had allocated the largest amounts of its ESF funds for CARSI activities to El Salvador, Guatemala, and Honduras (see table 8). Furthermore, USAID had disbursed approximately $51 million of ESF funds to support CARSI activities (see table 9). For fiscal year 2013, USAID officials explained that the agency has not yet been allocated funds from the Office of Management and Budget that Congress appropriated for fiscal year 2013. Therefore, the disbursement data provided below in table 9 for fiscal year 2013 are of funds allocated only in prior years, and table 8 reflects no allocations for fiscal year 2013.

Table 8: Economic Support Fund (ESF) Funding Allocated and Disbursed, Fiscal Year Appropriated, by the United States Agency for International Development (USAID) for Central America Regional Security Initiative (CARSI) Activities in Partner Countries, as of June 1, 2013

Dollars in thousands

Country[a]	2008	2009	2010	2011	2012	2013[b]	Total
El Salvador							
Allocated	4,000	2,750	5,744	7,850	9,800	0	3□,1□□
Unobligated balance	0	0	0	0	0	0	□
Unliquidated obligations[c]	0	150	425	5,848	9,800	0	1□,223
Disbursed[d]	4,000	2,600	5,319	2,002	0	0	13,□21
Guatemala							
Allocated	6,750	2,750	5,750	5,500	11,500	0	32,2□□
Unobligated balance	0	0	0	0	1,000[e]	0	1,□□□
Unliquidated obligations[c]	0	131	3,423	5,500	10,500	0	1□,□□□
Disbursed[d]	6,750	2,619	2,327	0	0	0	11,□□□
Honduras							
Allocated	2,000	4,250	5,500	7,425	16,500	0	3□,□7□
Unobligated balance	0	0	0	0	0	0	□
Unliquidated obligations[c]	0	1,040	2,333	6,757	16,484	0	2□,□1□
Disbursed[d]	2,000	3,342[f]	3,035[f]	668	16	0	□,□□1
Nicaragua							
Allocated	1,000	1,000	1,000	1,000	1,000	0	□,□□□
Unobligated balance	0	0	0	0	959[e]	0	□□□
Unliquidated obligations[c]	225	0	1,000	935	41	0	2,2□1
Disbursed[d]	775	1,000	0	65	0[g]	0	1,□□□
Panama							
Allocated	3,650	1,000	2,350	0	0	0	7,□□□
Unobligated balance	0	0	0	0	0	0	□
Unliquidated obligations[c]	0[g]	0	844	0	0	0	□□□

Dollars in thousands

Country[a]	FY2008	FY2009	FY2010	FY2011	FY2012	FY2013[b]	Total
Disbursed[d]	3,640	1,000	1506	0	0	0	6,146
Central America Regional Program[h]							
Allocated	0	0	0	5,224	2,500	0	7,724
Unobligated balance	0	0	0	0	0	0	0
Unliquidated obligations[c]	0	0	0	5,073	2,371	0	7,444
Disbursed[d]	0	0	0	151	129	0	280
Regional Sustainable Development Program[i]							
Allocated	2,600	4,250	1,300	501	5,200	0	13,851
Unobligated balance	0	0	6[e]	2[e]	4,660[e]	0	4,668
Unliquidated obligations[c]	33	316	36	150	331	0	866
Disbursed[d]	2,567	3,801[f]	1,390[f]	349	209	0	8,316

Source: GAO analysis of USAID data.

Notes: Amounts have been rounded to the nearest thousand and therefore may not sum to totals. USAID has 5 years from the time that the period of availability for obligation expires to disburse ESF funds.

[a]USAID has no assistance programs in Belize or Costa Rica, so neither country directly received ESF funding for CARSI activities from USAID. Also, as of fiscal year 2012, USAID's Mission in Panama is closed.

[b]Data cover 8 months of fiscal year 2013, from October 1, 2012, through June 1, 2013.

[c]According to State officials, unliquidated obligations for ESF are amounts that have been obligated but not disbursed or expensed and remain as uninvoiced or unpaid.

[d]According to State officials, disbursements for ESF are payments made by the agency to other parties using cash, checks, or electronic transfers.

[e]According to USAID officials, unobligated funds from fiscal years 2010 and 2011 are no longer available for obligation. Unobligated balances from fiscal year 2012 are available for obligation until September 30, 2013.

[f]According to USAID officials, a discrepancy of about $132,000 between Honduras and the Regional Sustainable Development Programs appears because there was a trade between the two operating units to ensure that all funds were obligated. At the end of fiscal year 2010, funds appropriated in 2009 for the Regional Sustainable Development Program were expiring and USAID's Bureau for Latin America and the Caribbean was not able to obligate them. These funds were transferred to USAID Honduras, which obligated them before they were going to expire. In exchange, an equal amount of 2010 funding to USAID Honduras was transferred back to the Regional Sustainable Development Program for obligation.

[g]Because we are presenting budget data in thousands of dollars, amounts under $1,000 are reported as zero. For Nicaragua the amount is $342 and for Panama $257.

[h]The Central America Regional Program is administered out of El Salvador; its location is advantageous for programming that supports the Central America Integration System (SICA), which is headquartered in El Salvador. SICA is the institutional framework for regional integration in Central America; it was created by Belize, Costa Rica, El Salvador, Guatemala, Honduras, Nicaragua, and Panama.

[i]The Regional Sustainable Development Program is administered out of Washington, D.C., and is targeted to assist the countries of El Salvador, Honduras, Guatemala, Nicaragua, and Panama.

Table □□□nite□ □tate□ Agenc□ □□r □nternati□nal □e□el□□ment □□A□□□c□n□mic □□□□□rt □□n□ □□□□□□□n□ing □□□i□cal □ear □i□□□re□t□ □□□□□rt Central America □egi□nal □ec□rit□ □nitiati□e □CA□□□□Acti□itie□ □a□ □□□□ne 1□2□13

Dollars in thousands							
C□□ntr□[a]	□□2□□□	□□2□□□	□□2□1□	□□2□11	□□2□12	□□2□13[b]	□□tal
El Salvador	0	0	2,031	3,082	5,137	3,671	13□21
Guatemala	0	0	311	3,973	5,034	2,379	11□□7
Honduras	0	0	850	2,001	2,728	3,481	□□□□□
Nicaragua	0	0	372	342	863	263	1□□□□
Panama	0	54	221	1,746	2,767	1,358	□□1□□
Central America Regional Program[c]	0	0	0	0	0	280	2□□
Regional Sustainable Program[d]	0	0	487	3,184	3,044	1,602	□317
CA□□□□□□ □□□A□□t□tal	□	□□	□272	1□32□	1□□□73	13□3□	□12□1

Source: GAO analysis of USAID data.

Notes: Amounts have been rounded to the nearest thousand and therefore may not sum to totals.

[a]USAID has no assistance programs in Belize or Costa Rica, so neither country directly received ESF funding for CARSI activities. Also, as of fiscal year 2012, USAID's Mission in Panama is closed.

[b]Data cover 8 months of fiscal year 2013, from October 1, 2012, through June 1, 2013.

[c]The Central America Regional Program is administered out of El Salvador; its location is advantageous for programming that supports the Central America Integration System (SICA), which is headquartered in El Salvador. SICA is the institutional framework for regional integration in Central America; it was created by Belize, Costa Rica, El Salvador, Guatemala, Honduras, Nicaragua, and Panama.

[d]The Regional Sustainable Development Program is administered out of Washington, D.C., and is targeted to assist the countries of El Salvador, Honduras, Guatemala, Nicaragua, and Panama.

Status of State's ESF Funding for CARSI Activities

As of June 1, 2013, State had allocated the largest amounts of its ESF funds for CARSI activities to Costa Rica, Belize, and Panama (see table 10).[2] Furthermore, State had disbursed approximately $10 million of ESF funding for CARSI activities (see table 11). In addition, State officials explained that the agency has not yet been allocated funds that Congress appropriated for fiscal year 2013. Therefore, the disbursement data provided below in table 11 for fiscal year 2013 are only of funds allocated in prior years, and table 10 reflects no allocations for fiscal year 2013.

[2]Costa Rica and Belize do not have USAID bilateral missions; therefore, State's Bureau of Western Hemisphere Affairs allotted funds to these embassies for obligation at post.

Table 1: Economic Support Fund Funding Allocated and Disbursed, Fiscal Year Appropriated, State toward Central America Regional Security Initiative (CARSI) Activities in Partner Countries, as of June 1, 2013

Dollars in thousands

Country	2008[a]	2009	2010	2011	2012	2013[b]	Total
Belize							
Allocated	468	450	300	600	500	0	2,318
Unobligated balance	0	22[c]	0	0	500[d]	0	522
Unliquidated obligations[e]	0	0	0	306	0	0	306
Disbursed[f]	468	428	300	294	0	0	1,490
Costa Rica							
Allocated	808	800	879	1,000	1,000	0	4,487
Unobligated balance	0	0	3[c]	0	1,000[d]	0	1,003
Unliquidated obligations[e]	0	0	0	100	0	0	100
Disbursed[f]	808	800	876	900	0	0	3,384
El Salvador							
Allocated	694	0	0	94	0	0	788
Unobligated balance	0	0	0	0	0	0	0
Unliquidated obligations[e]	0	0	0	56	0	0	56
Disbursed[f]	694	0	0	37	0	0	731
Guatemala							
Allocated	1,100	400	0	69	0	0	1,569
Unobligated balance	0	1[c]	0	0	0	0	1
Unliquidated obligations[e]	0	0	0	34	0	0	34
Disbursed[f]	1,100	399	0	34	0	0	1,533
Honduras							
Allocated	412	150	0	341	0	0	903
Unobligated balance	0	150[g]	0	0	0	0	150
Unliquidated obligations[e]	0	0	0	76	0	0	76
Disbursed[f]	412	0	0	264	0	0	676
Nicaragua							
Allocated	869	200	0	208	0	0	1,277
Unobligated balance	0	0	0	0	0	0	0
Unliquidated obligations[e]	0	0	0	42	0	0	42
Disbursed[f]	869	200	0	166	0	0	1,235
Panama							
Allocated	651	0	177	189	1,000	0	2,017
Unobligated balance	0	0	0	0	949[d]	0	949
Unliquidated obligations[e]	0	0	0	54	31	0	85

Dollars in thousands

Country	FY2008[a]	FY2009	FY2010	FY2011	FY2012	FY2013[b]	Total
Disbursed[f]	651	0	177	135	20	0	983
Regional[h]							
Allocated	0	0	0	0	1,000	0	1,000
Unobligated balance	0	0	0	0	1,000	0	1,000
Unliquidated obligations[e]	0	0	0	0	0	0	0
Disbursed[f]	0	0	0	0	0	0	0

Source: GAO analysis of State data.

Notes: Amounts have been rounded to the nearest thousand and therefore may not sum to totals. State has 5 years from the time that the period of availability for obligation expires to disburse ESF funds.

[a]For fiscal year 2008, $5 million of State CARSI ESF funding was made available for an Economic and Social Development Fund for Central America to help support educational exchange programs.

[b]Data cover 8 months of fiscal year 2013, from October 1, 2012, through June 1, 2013.

[c]According to State officials, reported unobligated amounts for fiscal years 2009 and 2010 have expired and are no longer available for obligation.

[d]According to State officials, unobligated balances for fiscal year 2012 are still available for obligation and are expected to be obligated by post in fiscal year 2013.

[e]According to State officials, unliquidated obligations for ESF are amounts that have been obligated but not disbursed or expensed and remain as uninvoiced or unpaid.

[f]According to State officials, disbursement for ESF are payments made by the agency to other parties using cash, checks, or electronic transfers.

[g]According to USAID officials, these funds were initially obligated and de-obligated at State and have since been returned to USAID.

[h]According to State officials, $1,000,000 of ESF funds from fiscal year 2012 are pending programming decisions with the Department and cannot be broken out by country. At the time of reporting these funds remain regional unobligated funds.

Table 11: State Economic Support Fund (ESF) Funding, by Fiscal Year Disbursed, to Support Central America Regional Security Initiative (CARSI) Activities, as of June 1, 2013

Dollars in thousands

Country	FY2008	FY2009	FY2010	FY2011	FY2012	FY2013[a]	Total
Belize	0	468	11	308	383	320	1,490
Costa Rica	0	808	0	1,304	875	397	3,384
El Salvador	0	694	0	0	0	37	731
Guatemala	0	1,100	0	399	34	0	1,533
Honduras	0	412	0	0	109	155	676
Nicaragua	0	869	0	133	100	133	1,235
Panama	0	651	0	82	172	78	983
CARSI ESF (State) total	0	5,002	11	2,226	1,673	1,120	10,032

Source: GAO analysis of State data.

Notes: Amounts have been rounded to the nearest thousand and therefore may not sum to totals.

[a]Data cover 8 months of fiscal year 2013, from October 1, 2012, through June 1, 2013.

Status of CARSI NADR Account Funds

State's Bureau of International Security and Nonproliferation and its Bureau of Counterterrorism administer CARSI NADR funds. NADR funds were allocated for Central American countries under the Mérida Initiative only for fiscal year 2008. NADR Export Control and Related Border Security (EXBS) and Counterterrorism (CT) funds were used to support activities in partner countries. As of June 1, 2013, the largest amount of funds had been allocated for NADR-EXBS activities, and 96 percent of those allocated funds had been disbursed (see table 12). Slightly more than $6 million of CARSI NADR-EXBS and NADR-CT funds were disbursed as of June 1, 2013 (see table 13). According to State officials, it is not possible to provide a country-by-country breakout of CARSI NADR-EXBS funds disbursed because the funds are intended for regional programming.

Table 12: Nonproliferation, Anti-terrorism, Demining, and Related Programs (NADR) Funding Allocated and Disbursed, by Fiscal Year Appropriated, to Fund Central America Regional Security Initiative (CARSI) Activities in Partner Countries, as of June 1, 2013

Dollars in thousands

	FY 2008		FY 2009	FY 2010	FY 2011	FY 2012	FY 2013	Total
Regional[a]	CT	EXBS						
Allocated	1,100	5,100	--	--	--	--	--	6,2[ ]
Unobligated balance	0	10[b]	--	--	--	--	--	1[ ]
Unliquidated obligations	0	176	--	--	--	--	--	17[ ]
Disbursed	1,100	4,914	--	--	--	--	--	6,01[ ]

Source: GAO analysis of State data.

Notes: Amounts have been rounded to the nearest thousand and therefore may not sum to totals. State has 5 years from the time the period of availability for obligation expires to disburse NADR funds. Dashes indicate "not applicable."

[a]NADR includes both NADR-Counterterrorism (CT) and NADR-Export Control and Related Border Security (EXBS) funding. NADR-EXBS programming is allocated, obligated, and tracked regionally for CARSI; therefore, State officials informed us that a break-out by country is not possible. CARSI NADR funds come from the Supplemental Appropriations Act, 2008, and were used to fund activities for Mérida-Central America.

[b]According to State officials, these funds were never obligated and the obligation period for these funds expired on September 30, 2009; therefore, these funds are no longer available for obligation. State officials explained that these funds were never obligated because contracts for NADR-EXBS activities were awarded on a competitive basis and actual costs were lower than estimated. These funds could not be applied to a different program prior to the obligation period expiring.

Table 13: □□□n□roliferation□Anti-terrorism□□emining an□ □elate□ Program□ □□A□□□□n□ing □□□□i□cal □ear □i□□□re□□t□ □□□□□rt Central America □egi□nal □ec□rit□ □nitiati□e □CA□□□□Acti□itie□□a□ □□□□ne 1□2□13

	□□2□□□	□□2□□□	□□2□1□	□□2□11	□□2□12	□□2□13[a]	□□tal
□A□□-□□□□[b]	0	974	2,283	712	334	611	□□□1□
□A□□-C□							
□□egi□nal □□tal□	0	376	103	385	219	15	1□□□□
Belize	0	4	0	179	151	15	3□□
Costa Rica	0	3	23	35	9	0	7□
El Salvador	0	14	5	34	10	0	□3
Guatemala	0	142	2	32	16	0	1□2
Honduras	0	133	0	14	19	0	1□□
Nicaragua	0	4	1	4	7	0	1□
Panama	0	0	5	32	7	0	□□
Costs of Grants to Organization of American States	0	77	67	55	0	0	1□□
CA□□□□A□□ t□tal	□	1□3□□	2□3□□	1□□□7	□□3	□2□	□□□12

Source: GAO analysis of State data.

Notes: Amounts have been rounded to the nearest thousand and therefore may not sum to totals. NADR includes both NADR-Counterterrorism (CT) and NADR-Export Control and Related Border Security (EXBS) funding. CARSI NADR funds came from the Supplemental Appropriations Act, 2008, and were used for activities for Mérida-Central America.

[a]Data cover 8 months of fiscal year 2013, from October 1, 2012, through June 1, 2013.

[b]NADR-EXBS programming is allocated regionally and not by country.

Appendix III: Status of Central America Regional Security Initiative Foreign Military Financing Account Funds

This appendix provides the status of Central America Regional Security Initiative (CARSI) Foreign Military Financing (FMF) funds as of June 1, 2013. Table 1 describes how U.S. agencies have allocated and committed FMF funds (by year of appropriation) toward activities in partner countries. The presentation of FMF allocations and commitments is different from presentations on allocations, obligations, and disbursements on the other CARSI accounts in appendix II because FMF funds are budgeted and tracked in a different way.

The Defense Security Cooperation Agency (DSCA) and the Defense Financing and Accounting Service (DFAS) are responsible for the financial systems that account for FMF funds, as well as tracking the implementation and disbursement of those funds. According to DSCA officials, FMF funds are obligated upon apportionment. Further, DSCA's system can only track FMF uncommitted and committed amounts, not unliquidated obligations or disbursements. DFAS tracks disbursements using the Defense Integrated Finance System; however, there is no direct link between the DSCA and DFAS systems, and the DFAS system does not track funding for specific initiatives, such as CARSI.

The Department of State (State) allocated close to $26 million of FMF funds for Central American countries for activities under the Mérida Initiative from fiscal years 2008 to 2010. From fiscal years 2008 to 2010, State allocated the largest amounts of these FMF funds to El Salvador, Costa Rica, and Panama. As of June 1, 2013, approximately 90 percent of the total allocated amount had been committed (see table 14).

Table 1: Central America Regional Security Initiative (CARSI) Foreign Military Financing (FMF) Funding Allocated and Committed, by Fiscal Year Appropriated, toward Central America Regional Security Initiative (CARSI) Activities in Partner Countries, as of June 1, 2013

Dollars in thousands

Country	2008	2009	2010	2011	2012	2013	Total
Belize							
Allocated	0	2,978	200	--	--	--	3,178
Unobligated balance	0	0	0	--	--	--	
Uncommitted[a]	0	0	0	--	--	--	
Committed[b]	0	2,978	200	--	--	--	3,178
Costa Rica							
Allocated	2,800	1,764	325	--	--	--	
Unobligated balance	0	0	0	--	--	--	

Country	2	2	201	2011	2012	2013	Total
Uncommitted[a]	0	311	0	--	--	--	311
Committed[b]	2,800	1,453	325	--	--	--	7
El Salvador							
Allocated	600	7,272	1,000	--	--	--	72
Unobligated balance	0	0	0	--	--	--	
Uncommitted[a]	0	917	426	--	--	--	13 3
Committed[b]	600	6,355	574	--	--	--	7 2
Guatemala							
Allocated	0	0	1,375	--	--	--	137
Unobligated balance	0	0	0	--	--	--	
Uncommitted[a]	0	0	0	--	--	--	
Committed[b]	0	0	1,375	--	--	--	137
Honduras							
Allocated	0	0	1,514	--	--	--	1 1
Unobligated balance	0	0	0	--	--	--	
Uncommitted[a]	0	0	0	--	--	--	
Committed[b]	0	0	1,514	--	--	--	1 1
Nicaragua							
Allocated	0	746	786	--	--	--	1 32
Unobligated balance	0	0	0	--	--	--	
Uncommitted[a]	0	146	786	--	--	--	32
Committed[b]	0	600	0	--	--	--	
Panama							
Allocated	600	2,159	1,800	--	--	--	
Unobligated balance	0	0	0	--	--	--	
Uncommitted[a]	0	104	0	--	--	--	1
Committed[b]	600	2,055	1,800	--	--	--	

Source: GAO analysis of State data.

Notes: Amounts have been rounded to the nearest thousand and therefore may not sum to totals. Dashes indicate "not applicable".

[a]For the purposes of this report, "uncommitted" amounts represent FMF obligations not yet committed for disbursement.

[b]For the purposes of this report, "committed" amounts include FMF funding that has been committed but not yet disbursed, and FMF funding that has been disbursed to a case.

Appendix IV: Comments from the U.S. Agency for International Development

FROM THE AMERICAN PEOPLE

SEP 10 2013

Charles Michael Johnson, Jr.
Director, International Affairs and Trade
Government Accountability Office
Washington, DC 20548

Dear Mr. Johnson:

    I am pleased to provide USAID's formal response to the Government Accountability Office (GAO) draft report entitled "CENTRAL AMERICA: U.S. Agencies Considered Various Factors in Funding Security Activities, but Need to Assess Progress in Achieving Interagency Objectives" (GAO-13-771).

    This letter, together with the enclosed USAID comments, are provided for incorporation as an appendix to the final report.

    Thank you for the opportunity to respond to the GAO draft report and for the courtesies extended by your staff in the conduct of this audit review.

Sincerely,

Angelique M. Crumbly
Assistant Administrator
Bureau for Management
U.S. Agency for International Development

Enclosure: a/s

USAID COMMENTS ON GAO DRAFT REPORT No. GAO-13-771

Recommendation 1: To help ensure that U.S. agencies have relevant information on the progress of the Central America Regional Security Initiative (CARSI) and related U.S. government activities, we recommend that the Secretary of State and the USAID Administrator direct their representatives on the Central America Interagency Working Group to work with the other members to assess the progress of CARSI and related U.S. government activities in achieving the objectives outlined in the U.S. government's interagency citizen security strategy for Central America.

USAID Response: USAID concurs with GAO's recommendation that the representatives on the Central America Interagency Working Group work closely together to assess the progress of CARSI and related U.S. government activities and to achieve the objectives outlined. This close coordination and consensus is a critical step to ensure continued progress toward our collective objectives. USAID agrees with the need to assess the performance metrics as laid out in the 2012 Interagency Strategy for Central America and commits to working with the Department of State and other U.S. government partners to determine the most appropriate metrics by which we can measure progress of CARSI programs. These metrics once approved will be shared with field missions to incorporate into their reporting mechanisms.

In addition, we would like to highlight that USAID's CARSI Impact Evaluation will conclude in 2014 and will serve as a useful tool to inform the future strategy and program priorities as the U.S. government progresses toward achieving greater impact as related to the metrics in the 2012 Interagency Strategy.

Appendix V: Comments from the Department of State

United States Department of State
Comptroller
P.O. Box 150008
Charleston, SC 29415-5008

SEP 10 2013

Dr. Loren Yager
Managing Director
International Affairs and Trade
Government Accountability Office
441 G Street, N.W.
Washington, D.C. 20548-0001

Dear Dr. Yager:

We appreciate the opportunity to review your draft report, "CENTRAL AMERICA: U.S. Agencies Considered Various Factors in Funding Security Activities but Need to Assess Progress in Achieving Interagency Objectives" GAO Job Code 320939.

The enclosed Department of State comments are provided for incorporation with this letter as an appendix to the final report.

If you have any questions concerning this response, please contact Thomas Wong, Strategic Planning Officer, Bureau of Western Hemisphere Affairs at (202) 647-5506.

Sincerely,

James L. Millette

cc: GAO – Charles M. Johnson, Jr.
        WHA – Roberta S. Jacobson
        State/OIG – Evelyn Klemstine

Department of State Comments on GAO Draft Report

<u>CENTRAL AMERICA: U.S. Agencies Considered Various Factors in
Funding Security Activities but Need to Assess Progress in Achieving
Interagency Objectives</u>
(GAO-13-771, GAO Code 320939)

The Department of State welcomes the opportunity to comment on the draft report *Central America: U.S. Agencies Considered Various Factors in Funding Security Activities but Need to Assess Progress in Achieving Interagency Objectives.*

The Department appreciates the professionalism with which GAO conducted program audit meetings, data collection, and analysis over the past year and GAO's stated willingness to incorporate the Department's technical comments into the final GAO report. The Department also thanks GAO for handling the sensitive details of the Central America Regional Security Initiative (CARSI) with care, acknowledging the vast array of programming involved in CARSI, and providing the GAO-Recommended Steps for Evaluation Design.

GAO's report makes one recommendation, that the Department work with other agencies on the Central America Interagency Working Group to assess the progress of CARSI and related U.S. government activities in achieving the objectives of the interagency citizen security strategy for Central America.

The Department concurs with GAO's recommendation. While CARSI activities are making progress towards the objectives outlined in the interagency citizen security strategy, the Department will seek to better capture the scope of this progress and use the information to inform policy. A results framework for CARSI will identify region-wide best practices and/or program areas that are not achieving the intended results. The Department will also seek, through an interagency process, to reexamine some of the objectives outlined in this strategy.

GAO's recommended five steps will guide an evaluation of the progress of dynamic and focused CARSI programming, aligned with the larger interagency strategy. The Bureau of International Narcotics and Law Enforcement Affairs (INL) is planning an evaluation of CARSI-funded activities in 2014.

Thank you again for the opportunity to respond to the GAO draft report and for the courtesies extended by your staff in the conduct of this review.

Appendix VI: GAO Contact and Staff Acknowledgments

GAO Contact	Charles Michael Johnson, Jr., (202) 512-7331 or johnsoncm@gao.gov
Staff Acknowledgments	In addition to the contact named above, Valérie L. Nowak (Assistant Director), Ian Ferguson, Marisela Perez, Ryan Vaughan, and Debbie Chung made key contributions to this report. Martin de Alteriis, Ashley Alley, Lynn Cothern, and Etana Finkler also provided assistance.

www.ingramcontent.com/pod-product-compliance
Lightning Source LLC
Chambersburg PA
CBHW080534290526
45790CB00006B/2402